Malnutrition

Other Books of Related Interest:

Opposing Viewpoints Series
Africa

At Issue Series
Fast Food

Current Controversies Series
Aid to Africa

"Congress shall make
no law . . . abridging
the freedom of speech,
or of the press."

First Amendment to the U.S. Constitution

The basic foundation of our democracy is the First Amendment guarantee of freedom of expression. The Opposing Viewpoints Series is dedicated to the concept of this basic freedom and the idea that it is more important to practice it than to enshrine it.

Malnutrition

Margaret Haerens, Book Editor

GREENHAVEN PRESS
A part of Gale, Cengage Learning

GALE
CENGAGE Learning™

Detroit • New York • San Francisco • New Haven, Conn • Waterville, Maine • London

Christine Nasso, *Publisher*
Elizabeth Des Chenes, *Managing Editor*

© 2009 Greenhaven Press, a part of Gale, Cengage Learning.

Gale and Greenhaven Press are registered trademarks used herein under license.

For more information, contact:
Greenhaven Press
27500 Drake Rd.
Farmington Hills, MI 48331-3535
Or you can visit our Internet site at gale.cengage.com

For product information and technology assistance, contact us at

Gale Customer Support, 1-800-877-4253
For permission to use material from this text or product, submit all requests online at www.cengage.com/permissions

Further permissions questions can be emailed to permissionrequest@cengage.com

Articles in Greenhaven Press anthologies are often edited for length to meet page requirements. In addition, original titles of these works are changed to clearly present the main thesis and to explicitly indicate the author's opinion. Every effort is made to ensure that Greenhaven Press accurately reflects the original intent of the authors. Every effort has been made to trace the owners of copyrighted material.

Cover photograph reproduced by image copyright © Dmitri Mikitenko, 2009. Used under license from Shutterstock.com.

LIBRARY OF CONGRESS CATALOGING-IN-PUBLICATION DATA

Malnutrition / Margaret Haerens, book editor.
  p. cm. -- (Opposing viewpoints)
  Includes bibliographical references and index.
  ISBN 978-0-7377-4384-5 (hardcover)
  ISBN 978-0-7377-4383-8 (pbk.)
  1. Food relief. 2. Malnutrition. 3. Nutrition policy. 4. Food supply. I. Haerens, Margaret.
  HV696.F6M343 2009
  362.196'39--dc22
                                                        2008045605

Printed in the United States of Americ
1 2 3 4 5 6 7 13 12 11 10 09

Contents

Chapter 3: Who Should Help Alleviate Malnutrition?

Chapter 4: What Policies Will Alleviate Malnutrition?

Why Consider
Opposing Viewpoints?

> *"The only way in which a human being
> can make some approach to knowing the
> whole of a subject is by hearing what
> can be said about it by persons of every
> variety of opinion and studying all
> modes in which it can be looked at by
> every character of mind. No wise man
> ever acquired his wisdom in any mode
> but this."*
>
> John Stuart Mill

In our media-intensive culture it is not difficult to find differing opinions. Thousands of newspapers and magazines and dozens of radio and television talk shows resound with differing points of view. The difficulty lies in deciding which opinion to agree with and which "experts" seem the most credible. The more inundated we become with differing opinions and claims, the more essential it is to hone critical reading and thinking skills to evaluate these ideas. Opposing Viewpoints books address this problem directly by presenting stimulating debates that can be used to enhance and teach these skills. The varied opinions contained in each book examine many different aspects of a single issue. While examining these conveniently edited opposing views, readers can develop critical thinking skills such as the ability to compare and contrast authors' credibility, facts, argumentation styles, use of persuasive techniques, and other stylistic tools. In short, the Opposing Viewpoints Series is an ideal way to attain the higher-level thinking and reading skills so essential in a culture of diverse and contradictory opinions.

In addition to providing a tool for critical thinking, Opposing Viewpoints books challenge readers to question their own strongly held opinions and assumptions. Most people form their opinions on the basis of upbringing, peer pressure, and personal, cultural, or professional bias. By reading carefully balanced opposing views, readers must directly confront new ideas as well as the opinions of those with whom they disagree. This is not to simplistically argue that everyone who reads opposing views will—or should—change his or her opinion. Instead, the series enhances readers' understanding of their own views by encouraging confrontation with opposing ideas. Careful examination of others' views can lead to the readers' understanding of the logical inconsistencies in their own opinions, perspective on why they hold an opinion, and the consideration of the possibility that their opinion requires further evaluation.

Evaluating Other Opinions

To ensure that this type of examination occurs, Opposing Viewpoints books present all types of opinions. Prominent spokespeople on different sides of each issue as well as well-known professionals from many disciplines challenge the reader. An additional goal of the series is to provide a forum for other, less known, or even unpopular viewpoints. The opinion of an ordinary person who has had to make the decision to cut off life support from a terminally ill relative, for example, may be just as valuable and provide just as much insight as a medical ethicist's professional opinion. The editors have two additional purposes in including these less known views. One, the editors encourage readers to respect others' opinions—even when not enhanced by professional credibility. It is only by reading or listening to and objectively evaluating others' ideas that one can determine whether they are worthy of consideration. Two, the inclusion of such viewpoints encourages the important critical thinking skill of objectively evaluating an author's credentials and bias. This evaluation will illuminate an author's reasons for taking a particular stance on an issue and will aid in readers' evaluation of the author's ideas.

It is our hope that these books will give readers a deeper understanding of the issues debated and an appreciation of the complexity of even seemingly simple issues when good and honest people disagree. This awareness is particularly important in a democratic society such as ours in which people enter into public debate to determine the common good. Those with whom one disagrees should not be regarded as enemies but rather as people whose views deserve careful examination and may shed light on one's own.

Thomas Jefferson once said that "difference of opinion leads to inquiry, and inquiry to truth." Jefferson, a broadly educated man, argued that "if a nation expects to be ignorant and free . . . it expects what never was and never will be." As individuals and as a nation, it is imperative that we consider the opinions of others and examine them with skill and discernment. The Opposing Viewpoints Series is intended to help readers achieve this goal.

David L. Bender and Bruno Leone,
Founders

Introduction

> *"Proper nutrition is a powerful good: People who are well nourished are more likely to be healthy, productive and able to learn. Good nutrition benefits families, their communities and the world as a whole."*
>
> *"Malnutrition is, by the same logic, devastating. It plays a part in more than a third of all child deaths in developing countries. It blunts the intellect, saps the productivity of everyone it touches and perpetuates poverty."*
>
> *The United Nations*
> *Children's Fund (UNICEF)*

Although malnutrition remains a deadly problem in many areas of the world, there are constantly new initiatives to try to alleviate it. In sub-Saharan Africa in the mid-1990s, the rapid population growth was fast outstripping the static production of rice. Nearly 240 million people in West Africa depend on rice as the primary source of food energy and protein in their diets. Farmers in the region were faced with a tough choice: grow Asian rice, which is a high-yield species that is poorly adapted to Africa's growing conditions; or grow African rice, which is better adapted to the sub-Saharan climate and soil but offers a much lower yield. It was soon clear that neither choice was meeting the escalating demand for rice, and governments in the region were forced to import rice to feed their people at the cost of approximately $1 billion annually.

A plan of action was formed, and a group was established—the New Rice for Africa (NERICA) project. Funded by the African Development Bank, the Japanese government, and the United Nations Development Program, NERICA used agricultural technology to improve the yield of African rice. The West Africa Rice Development Association (WARDA), an autonomous intergovernmental research association made up of members from several African states, developed hybrid varieties of rice—a cross between the Asian and African rice—that are high yielding, drought resistant, and protein rich. Over the past five years, these hybrid varieties have been planted in several West African countries, including Congo Brazzaville, Cote d'Ivoire, the Democratic Republic of the Congo, Guinea, Kenya, Mali, Nigeria, Togo, and Uganda, with amazing success. In 2006, it was estimated that NERICA rice varieties were being grown on more than 200,000 hectares of land in West Africa.

Today, some eighteen varieties of the hybrid species have been distributed to rice farmers across sub-Saharan Africa, resulting in improved nutrition and a decrease in malnutrition in several countries in Africa. For the first time, many African farmers have been able to not only produce enough rice for their families, but also take their excess to market and turn a tidy profit. It has allowed there to be food security in areas where there was little. Standards of living have improved, with farmers able to provide conveniences for their families such as plumbing, beds, and investment in new crops and farming equipment to further help their annual yield.

The NERICA project is an impressive success story that could not have been possible without the generous contribution of private and public investment. These global partnerships are springing up all over the world to address major global problems like hunger and malnutrition. National, regional, and local governments; private corporations; international governmental organizations; and non-governmental organizations are discovering that coming together to find aggressive and creative solutions to the devastating problem of malnutrition benefits everyone and is an imperative step to alleviate such a pernicious problem.

Unfortunately, for every success story like the NERICA project, there is a place where natural disasters, drought, conflict, poverty and other factors result in the region plummeting into hunger and malnutrition. Some areas seem to always be suffering, usually because of constant war or government incompetence or indifference.

There are far too few success stories like the NERICA project, particularly when we consider the resources and technology in the modern world. Global partnerships are making a positive difference, but more are needed to confront the issue fully. In a world where food is abundant, we have to wonder why there are still starving and malnourished people in the world and why, despite all our advancements, we have not been able to fully and successfully address the problem.

The authors of the viewpoints presented in *Opposing Viewpoints: Malnutrition* discuss many of these issues in the following chapters: How Serious Is the Problem of Malnutrition? What Are the Root Causes of Malnutrition? Who Should Help Alleviate Malnutrition? What Policies Will Help Alleviate Malnutrition? The information in this volume will provide insight into why malnutrition is such a severe global problem and what the worldwide community is doing to alleviate it.

How Serious Is the Problem of Malnutrition?

Chapter Preface

Malnutrition is a worldwide problem that results in the deaths of millions of people—especially children—every year, and is considered one of the gravest threats that exists to global health. There are generally acknowledged to be two forms of malnutrition: undernutrition and overnutrition. Adults and children who are undernourished do not have the appropriate amount or types of nutrients that comprise a healthy diet for an extended period of time. They may not have enough food; are not eating a balanced diet rich in vitamins and minerals; or their bodies cannot absorb nutrients in an efficient manner. Undernutrition in children can result in stunted growth, reduced cognitive abilities, and vulnerability to starvation, disease, and infection. Prolonged undernourishment can result in death. In fact, the World Health Organization (WHO) reported that it is by far the biggest contributor to child mortality cases around the world. WHO also contends that more than 36 million people died of hunger or diseases due to deficiencies in micronutrients in 2006.

Overnutrition results from overeating or excessive intake of specific nutrients. Obese people eat too many calories, consume an excessive amount of certain nutrients, or eat too much unhealthy food lacking in nutrients. The results of overnutrition are serious. Obesity can lead to chronic conditions such as heart disease and diabetes. However, some observers do not believe that obesity should be considered the serious threat that global malnutrition is. They view the problem as a correctable one: if behavior changes, the problem disappears.

There are two common forms of malnutrition: protein-energy malnutrition (PEM), which refers to a lack of energy and proteins in the body; and micronutrient malnutrition, which is defined as the lack of essential nutrients, such as Vitamin A (which helps fight diseases), iron, and iodine. Both of these forms of malnutrition are considered a serious threat to global public health.

The viewpoints collected in the following chapter will explore the severity of undernutrition and overnutrition in the United States and in the global community. Although everyone agrees that malnutrition is a major problem and should be addressed, some disagree on how severe it is, on whether the statistics are correct, and as to whether the issue has been exaggerated.

*"In this era relatively few people actu-
ally die from starvation. . . . Most instead become chronically malnourished
and then are plagued by a variety of
diseases that shorten their lives or make
them more miserable."*

Global Malnutrition Is
a Severe Problem

Fred Magdoff

*Fred Magdoff is professor emeritus of plant and soil science at
the University of Vermont in Burlington and a director of the
Monthly Review Foundation. In the following viewpoint, Magdoff surveys the scope of the widespread food crisis that has left
billions of people around the world suffering from chronic and
severe malnutrition.*

As you read, consider the following questions:

1. According to United Nations estimates, how many
   people in the world suffer from chronic hunger?
2. How many billion people does the author estimate are
   "food insecure"?

Fred Magdoff, "The World Food Crisis: Sources and Solutions," *Monthly Review*, May
2008. Copyright © 2008 by Monthly Review Press. Reproduced by permission of
Monthly Review Foundation.

3. What are the two separate food crises that the author references?

An acute food crisis has struck the world in 2008. This is on top of a longer-term crisis of agriculture and food that has already left billions hungry and malnourished. In order to understand the full, dire implications of what is happening today it is necessary to look at the interaction between these short-term and long-term crises. Both crises arise primarily from the for-profit production of food, fiber, and now biofuels, and the rift between food and people that this inevitably generates.

"Routine" Hunger Before the Current Crisis

Of the more than 6 billion people living in the world today, the United Nations estimates that close to 1 billion suffer from chronic hunger. But this number, which is only a crude estimate, leaves out those suffering from vitamin and nutrient deficiencies and other forms of malnutrition. The total number of food insecure people who are malnourished or lacking critical nutrients is probably closer to 3 billion—about half of humanity. The severity of this situation is made clear by the United Nations estimate of over a year ago that approximately 18,000 children die *daily* as a direct or indirect consequence of malnutrition.

Lack of production is rarely the reason that people are hungry. This can be seen most clearly in the United States, where despite the production of more food than the population needs, hunger remains a significant problem. According to the U.S. Department of Agriculture, in 2006, over 35 million people lived in food-insecure households, including 13 million children. Due to a lack of food, adults living in over 12 million households could not eat balanced meals and in over 7 million families, someone had smaller portions or skipped meals. In close to 5 million families, children did not get enough to eat at some point during the year.

In poor countries too, it is not unusual for large supplies of wasted and misallocated food to exist in the midst of widespread and persistent hunger. A few years ago [in 2002] a *New York Times* article had a story with the following headline "Poor in India Starve as Surplus Wheat Rots." As a *Wall Street Journal* headline put it in 2004 "Want Amid Plenty, An Indian Paradox: Bumper Harvests and Rising Hunger."

No "Right to Food"

Hunger and malnutrition generally are symptoms of a larger underlying problem—poverty in an economic system that recognizes, as Rachel Carson put it, no other gods but those of profit and production. Food is treated in almost all of the world's countries as just another commodity, like clothes, automobiles, pencils, books, diamond jewelry, and so on. People are not considered to have a right to purchase any particular commodity, and no distinction is made in this respect between necessities and luxuries. Those who are rich can afford to purchase anything they want while the poor are often not able to procure even their basic needs. Under capitalist relations, people have no right to an adequate diet, shelter, and medical attention. As with other commodities, people without what economists call "effective demand" cannot buy sufficient nutritious food. Of course, lack of "effective demand" in this case means that the poor don't have enough money to buy the food they need.

Humans have a "biological demand" for food—we all need food, just as we need water and air, to continue to live. It is a systematic fact of capitalist society that many are excluded from fully meeting this biological need. It's true that some wealthy countries, especially those in Europe, do help feed the poor, but the very way capitalism functions inherently creates a lower strata of society that frequently lacks the basics for human existence. In the United States there are a variety of government initiatives—such as food stamps and school lunch programs—aimed at feeding the poor. Yet, the funding for these programs does not come close to meeting the needs of the poor, and various charities fight an uphill battle trying to make up the difference.

In this era relatively few people actually die from starvation, aside from the severe hunger induced by wars and dislocations. Most instead become chronically malnourished and then are plagued by a variety of diseases that shorten their lives or make them more miserable. The scourge of malnutrition impedes children's mental and physical development, harming them for the rest of their lives.

The Acute and Growing Crisis: The Great Hunger of 2008

At this moment in history, there are, in addition to the "routine" hunger discussed above, two separate global food crises occurring simultaneously. The severe and acute crisis, about two years old [as of 2008], is becoming worse day by day and it is this one that we'll discuss first. The severity of the current crisis cannot be overstated. It has rapidly increased the number of people around the globe that are malnourished. Although statistics of increased hunger during the past year are not yet available, it is clear that many will die prematurely or be harmed in other ways. As usual, it will be the young, the old, and the infirm that will suffer the worst effects of the Great Hunger of 2008. The rapid and simultaneous rise in the world prices for all the basic food crops—corn (maize), wheat, soybeans, rice, and cooking oils—along with many other crops, is having a devastating effect on an increasing portion of humanity.

The increases in the world market prices over the past few years have been nothing short of astounding. The prices of the sixty agricultural commodities traded on the world market increased 37 percent last year and 14 percent in 2006. Corn prices began their rise in the early fall of 2006 and

Facts and Figures on Health

- Poor nutrition and calorie deficiencies cause nearly one in three people to die prematurely or have disabilities, according to the World Health Organization (WHO).

- Pregnant women, new mothers who breastfeed infants, and children are among the most at risk of undernourishment.

- In 2005, about 10.1 million children died before they reached their fifth birthday. Almost all of these deaths occurred in developing countries, three-fourths of them in sub-Saharan Africa and South Asia, the two regions that also suffer from the highest rates of hunger and malnutrition.

Bread for the World,
"Hunger Facts: International,"
June 6, 2007. www.bread.org.

within months had soared by some 70 percent. Wheat and soybean prices also skyrocketed during this time and are now at record levels. The prices for cooking oils (mainly made from soybeans and oil palm)—an essential foodstuff in many poor countries—have rocketed up as well. Rice prices have also risen over 100 percent in the last year.

The reasons for these soaring food prices are fairly clear. First, there are a number of issues related directly or indirectly to the increase in petroleum prices. In the United States, Europe, and many other countries this has brought a new emphasis on growing crops that can be used for fuel—called biofuels (or agrofuels). Thus, producing corn to make ethanol or soybean and palm oil to make diesel fuel is in direct competition with the use of these crops for food. Last year over 20 percent of the entire corn crop in the United States was used to produce ethanol—a process that does not yield much additional energy over that which goes into producing it. (It is estimated that over the next decade about one-third of the U.S. corn crop will be devoted to ethanol production.) Additionally, many of the inputs for large-scale commercial agricultural production are based on petroleum and natural gas—from building and running tractors and harvesting equipment to producing fertilizers and pesticides and drying crops for storage. The price of nitrogen fertilizer, the most commonly used fertilizer worldwide, is directly tied to the price of energy because it takes so much energy to produce.

A second cause of the increase in prices of corn and soybeans and soy cooking oil is the increasing demand for meat among the middle class in Latin America and Asia, especially China. The use of maize and soy to feed cattle, pigs, and poultry has risen sharply to satisfy this demand. The world's total meat supply was 71 million tons in 1961. In 2007, it was estimated to be 284 million tons. Per capita consumption has more than doubled over that period. In the developing world, it rose twice as fast, doubling in the last twenty years alone. Feeding grain to more and more animals is putting growing pressure on grain stores. Feeding grain to produce meat is a very inefficient way of providing people with either calories or protein. It is especially wasteful for animals such as cows—with digestive systems that can derive energy from cellulose—because they can obtain all of their nutrition from pastures and will grow well without grain, although more slowly. Cows are not efficient converters of corn or soy to meat—to yield a pound of meat, cows require eight pounds of corn; pigs, five; and chickens, three.

A third reason for the big jump in world food prices is that a few key countries that were self-sufficient—that is, did not import foods, although plenty of people suffered from hunger—are now importing large quantities of food. As a farm analyst in New Delhi says [as quoted in *VOA News* in 2008], "When countries like India start importing food, then the world prices zoom. . . . If India and China are both turning into bigger importers, shifting from food self-sufficiency as recently we have seen in India, then the global prices are definitely going to rise still further, which will mean the era of cheaper food has now definitely gone away." Part of the reason for the pressure on rice prices is the loss of farmland to other uses such as various development projects—some 7 million acres in China and 700,000 acres in Vietnam. In addition, rice yields per acre in Asia have reached a plateau. There has been no per acre increase for ten years and yield increases are not expected in the near future. . . .

The Long-Term Food Crisis

As critical as the short-term food crisis is—demanding immediate world notice as well as attention within every country—the long-term, structural crisis is even more important. The latter has existed for decades and contributes to, and is reinforced by, today's acute food crisis. Indeed, it is this underlying structural crisis of agriculture and food in third world societies which constitutes the real reason that the immediate food crisis is so severe and so difficult to surmount within the system.

There has been a huge migration of people out of the countryside to the cities of the third world. They leave the countryside because they lack access to land. Often their land has been stolen as a result of the inroads of agribusiness, while they are also forced from the land by low prices they have historically received for their products and threats against campesino lives. They move to cities seeking a better life but what they find is a very hard existence—life in slums with extremely high unemployment and underemployment. Most will try to scrape by in the "informal" economy by buying things and then selling them in small quantities. Of the half of humanity that lives in cities (3 billion), some 1 billion, or one-third of city dwellers, live in slums. The chairman of a district in Lagos, Nigeria described it as follows: "We have a massive growth in population with a stagnant or shrinking economy. Picture this city ten, twenty years from now. This is not the urban poor—this is the new urban destitute." A long *New Yorker* article [in 2006] on Lagos ended on a note of extreme pessimism: "The really disturbing thing about Lagos' pickers and vendors is that their lives have essentially nothing to do with ours. They scavenge an existence beyond the margins of macroeconomics. They are, in the harsh terms of globalization, superfluous."

One of the major factors pushing this mass and continuing migration to the cities—in addition to being landless or forced off land—is the difficulty to make a living as a small farmer. This has been made especially difficult, as countries have implemented the "neoliberal" policies recommended or mandated by the IMF [International Monetary Fund], the World Bank, and even some of the western NGOs [non-governmental organizations] working in the poor countries of the third world. The neoliberal ideology holds that the so-called free market should be allowed to work its magic. Through the benign sanctions of the "invisible hand," it is said, the economy will function most efficiently and will be highly productive. But in order for the market to be "free" governments must stop interfering.

"*We can be all too sure that scores of millions in our world suffer from heart-rending, life-impairing hunger. But exaggerating the current scope of the problem, and minimizing the strides we have already made against it, will serve no worthy purpose.*"

The Problem of Global Malnutrition Is Exaggerated

Nicholas N. Eberstadt

Nicholas Eberstadt is a member of the Harvard University Center for Population and Developmental Studies and a Henry Wendt Scholar in political economy at the American Enterprise Institute. He has written extensively on poverty, foreign aid, and health issues. In the following viewpoint, he argues that efforts to alleviate hunger and malnutrition around the world are hindered by the tendency to exaggerate the problem.

As you read, consider the following questions:

1. How many people were estimated to be undernourished in 1996, according to evidence presented at the World Food Summit?

Nicholas N. Eberstadt, "Starved for Ideas: Misconceptions That Hinder the Battle against World Hunger," *American Enterprise Institute for Public Policy Research*, November 25, 1996. Reproduced by permission.

2. According to the author, how are recent international studies that attempt to quantify global hunger and malnutrition flawed?

3. What are meaningful factors the author introduces to assess nutritional progress on a global scale?

There is scarcely a nobler quest in the world than the search for solutions to the continuing tragedies of starvation and famine. But perhaps in no other humanitarian venture do people so mistake good intentions for good policy. The subject of world hunger can cause the vision of ordinarily brilliant intellectuals, learned academicians, and clearheaded statesmen suddenly to blur. All around the world, specialists and policy makers continue to entertain beliefs and accept premises about the world food situation that are demonstrably, often glaringly, invalid—and, therefore, life-threatening.

To a strange and disturbing degree, modern international man is, quite literally, starved for ideas. Widely accepted misconceptions, stubborn *idées fixes*, and crude ideological notions about the nature of hunger and famine in the modern world are impeding the quest to achieve food security for all. Guided—or more exactly, misguided—by fundamentally flawed assessments of the prevalence and causes of global hunger, we cannot hope to attain satisfactory results. At best, our well-meaning efforts will be merely ineffective; at worst, we risk making bad conditions worse and injuring our intended beneficiaries.

Modern-day myths about the world food problem are legion [including one that] concerns the current dimensions of the hunger problem. . . .

Determining the Scope of World Hunger

According to a large body of major studies by reputable and authoritative organizations, the magnitude of the global malnutrition problem in the modern era is vast—so vast as to be

29

almost incomprehensible. According to some of these studies, moreover, the problem has been worsening over time.

In 1950, Lord Boyd-Orr, the first director general of the United Nations [UN] Food and Agricultural Organization (FAO), warned that "a lifetime of malnutrition and actual hunger is the lot of at least two-thirds of mankind." Thirty years later, a United States Presidential Commission on World Hunger concluded that "this world hunger problem is getting worse rather than better. There are more hungry people than ever before." In 1991, the U.N. World Food Council declared that "the number of chronically hungry people in the world continues to grow." And at the World Food Summit held . . . [in 1996] in Rome, an official document put the undernourished population of the world at well over 800 million. That figure suggests that one out of five persons from developing countries was suffering from chronic undernutrition in the early 1990s.

By such soundings, we would seem to have made no relative progress whatever against third world hunger over the past generation. And given the growth of population in the less developed regions, the absolute number of hungry people in the world would appear to have increased tremendously in recent decades.

A distressing and disheartening picture, no doubt. But there is one small thing wrong with this picture: It is empirically false. Astonishing as it may sound to the nonspecialist, *every major international study that has attempted to quantify global hunger over the past two generations is demonstrably and deeply flawed.*

Flawed Malnutrition Studies

Using the methods employed in any one of these studies, it would be impossible to derive an accurate impression of the global hunger situation. And the conditions under which some of the studies were prepared were far from ideal. For citizens

Child Mortality at Record Low

For the first time since record keeping began in 1960, the number of deaths of young children around the world has fallen below 10 million a year, according to figures from the United Nations Children's Fund [UNICEF being released today [September 13, 2007].

This public health triumph has arisen, UNICEF officials said, partly from campaigns against measles, malaria and bottle-feeding, and partly from improvements in the economies of most of the world outside Africa.

Donald G. McNeil Jr.,
"Child Mortality at Record Low: Further Drop Seen,"
New York Times, *September 13, 2007. www.nytimes.com.*

and policy makers committed to charting a course against world hunger, these studies offer a distorted and misleading map.

The flaws are sometimes quite technical, but they are never difficult to describe. In every instance, they are due to questionable and unsupported assumptions about individual nutritional needs in large populations, and equally questionable assumptions about the correspondence between national food supplies and individual food intake.

Malnutrition is an affliction suffered by individuals. Short of clinical or biomedical examination, there is no reliable way to determine a person's health or nutritional status. Because they lack this person-by-person information, these studies draw clumsy inferences about individual well-being. They cannot cope with such exacting, but important, issues as whether individuals with lower caloric intake have lower than average caloric requirements; whether individual metabolic efficiency adjusts in response to changes in the nutritional supply; or whether individuals predicted by their models to be undernourished actually suffer from identifiable nutritional afflictions. To pose these questions is not to presuppose an answer to them; it is simply to discharge a basic duty of careful inquiry.

An Example of a Flawed Study

Sometimes the results of these hunger studies can be dismissed after even the most casual inspection. In 1980, the World Bank published a paper purporting to show that three-fourths of the population of the less developed regions suffered from "caloric deficits." This ominous conclusion was reached by a chain of dubious suppositions, the final and most spectacular of which was that anyone receiving less than the average "recommended dietary allowance" was underfed. In truth, about half of any population will need less than the average allowance; that is the meaning of the word "average." Consequently, this model could only generate nonsense numbers: Its computations suggested, among other things, that nearly half the people in prosperous Hong Kong were getting too little food!

To their credit, the World Bank researchers on this particular project recognized that their work failed the "reality test" and went back to the drawing board to improve their product. Unfortunately, others working on the problem have not always met the same standards of intellectual accountability. Lord Boyd-Orr, for example, did not at the time explain the method underlying his now-famous estimate of the prevalence of world hunger. After reviewing contemporary data, one of the leading agricultural experts of the day, Merrill K. Bennett, surmised that this estimate might actually be an elementary computational mistake—a misreading of the figures in two particular columns of a particular table. The Food and

Agricultural Organization, which prepared the figures Lord Boyd-Orr used, never replied to Bennett's inquiry and has never offered substantiating evidence for Boyd-Orr's assertion. Other estimates about world hunger from the same organization have remained similarly protected against outside inspection: Most of the data and calculations in the first three FAO World Food Surveys, for example, are still unavailable to the public. In its more recent studies, the organization's determination of the number of calories an individual needs for nourishment has been rising steadily over time. Why? These upward revisions do not seem to reflect any obvious changes in the scientific consensus concerning nutritional norms. But they do produce higher totals for any given estimate of the number of hungry people in the world.

A Different Story

If we could only for a moment extricate ourselves from this numerical house of mirrors, we would see that there are indeed meaningful data that bear upon the actual nutritional status of humanity, and that they tell a rather different story.

Household spending patterns in less developed regions, for example, can reveal how the poor assess *their own* nutritional status. If a family treats food as a "superior good"—that is to say, if an increase in income raises the overall share of the household budget going to food—it renders a telling judgment that its members have had too little to eat. By this criterion, the incidence of serious hunger in the world would be far lower than the Food and Agricultural Organization currently suggests: about two-thirds lower in some years for India, to take one example.

Mortality rates, for their part, offer a direct and unambiguous measure of the material condition of any population. It is clear that the so-called third world has experienced a revolution in health conditions over the past generation. According to the U.N. Secretariat, life expectancy at birth there rose by an average of almost a decade and a half between the early 1960s and the early 1990s. And over that same period, infant mortality there is estimated to have dropped nearly by half. Can one really imagine that such dramatic gains were entirely unaccompanied by nutritional progress?

The truth is that a precise and reliable method for estimating the incidence and severity of worldwide malnutrition has yet to be devised. We can be all too sure that scores of millions in our world suffer from heart-rending, life-impairing hunger. But exaggerating the current scope of the problem, and minimizing the strides we have already made against it, will serve no worthy purpose. Hungry populations certainly do not benefit from such misapprehensions. In an age of "compassion fatigue," these misrepresentations of reality tend instead to discourage action by depicting the problem as almost insurmountably large. And to make matters worse, they may direct available humanitarian resources away from the places where they might have made the biggest difference.

> "A high number of food insecure house-
> holds in a nation with our economic
> plenty means that the fruits of our
> economy, and the benefits of public and
> private programs for needy people, are
> not yet reaching millions of low-
> income people who are at great risk."

Malnutrition Is a Serious Problem in the United States

Food Research and Action Center

*The Food Research and Action Center (FRAC) is a nonprofit or-
ganization working to improve public policies to eradicate hunger and undernutrition in the United States. FRAC works with
hundreds of national, state, and local nonprofit organizations,
public agencies, and corporations to address hunger and poverty.
In the following viewpoint, the organization offers statistics that
show how pervasive hunger and food insecurity are in the United
States. The authors maintain that while severe starvation and
malnutrition are rare in this country because of federal, state,
and local intervention, some Americans do experience chronic
mild undernutrition, which can have harmful effects on child
development, productivity, and physical and psychological health.*

Food Research and Action Center, "Hunger and Food Insecurity in the United States,"
FRAC.org, January 17, 2007. Reproduced by permission.

As you read, consider the following questions:

1. According to the U.S. Department of Agriculture, how many Americans live in food-insecure households?
2. How many of these are children?
3. What groups are the greatest risk of going hungry or being food insecure, according to the U.S. Census Bureau survey?

One of the most disturbing and extraordinary aspects of life in this very wealthy country is the persistence of hunger. The U.S. Department of Agriculture (USDA) reported that in 2006:

- 35.5 million people lived in households considered to be food insecure.

- Of these 35.5 million, 22.9 million are adults (10.4 percent of all adults) and 12.6 million are children (17.2 percent of all children).

- The number of people in the worst-off households increased to 11.1 from 10.8 in 2005. This increase in the number of people in the worst-off category is consistent with other studies and the Census Bureau poverty data, which show worsening conditions for the poorest Americans.

- Black (21.8 percent) and Hispanic (19.5 percent) households experienced food insecurity at far higher rates than the national average.

- The ten states with the highest food insecurity rates in 2006 were Mississippi, New Mexico, Texas, South Carolina, Oklahoma, Utah, Louisiana, Arkansas, Kentucky, and Arizona.

Hunger and Food Insecurity in the United States

Very simply, hunger is defined as the uneasy or painful sensation caused by lack of food. When we talk about hunger in America, we refer to the ability of people to obtain sufficient food for their household. Some people may find themselves skipping meals or cutting back on the quality or quantity of food they purchase at the stores. This recurring and involuntary lack of access to food can lead to malnutrition over time.

In some developing nations where famine is widespread, hunger manifests itself as severe and very visible clinical malnutrition. In the United States, hunger manifests itself, generally, in a less severe form. This is in part because established programs—like the federal nutrition programs—help to provide a safety net for many low-income families. While starvation seldom occurs in this country, children and adults do go hungry and chronic mild undernutrition does occur when financial resources are low. The mental and physical changes that accompany inadequate food intakes can have harmful effects on learning, development, productivity, physical and psychological health, and family life.

The government uses two main terms to describe the levels of hunger problems we typically face in the United States. Food security is a term used to describe what our nation should be seeking for all its people—assured access at all times to enough food for an active, healthy life, with no need for recourse to emergency food sources or other extraordinary coping behaviors to meet basic food needs. In a nation as affluent as ours, this is a readily achievable goal. Food insecurity refers to the lack of access to enough food to fully meet basic needs at all times due to lack of financial resources. There are different levels of food insecurity.

Measuring Hunger and Food Insecurity

In the 1980s, due to a combination of cuts in public welfare programs and a recession, many communities across the country experienced an enormous increase in demand for emergency food, often among families with children. Community leaders wanted to document this growing problem so that policy makers would recognize its severity and do something about the hunger they were seeing. Out of this expressed need developed FRAC's [Food Research and Action Center] Community Childhood Hunger Identification Project (CCHIP), the first nationwide survey measuring the extent of hunger among families with children, the results of which were released in 1991 and 1995.

At the same time that CCHIP was being conducted, FRAC worked with a broad coalition of national organizations to get national nutrition monitoring legislation through Congress—legislation that required the federal government, among other things, to develop a measure of food insufficiency that could be added to the national nutrition monitoring system. Using CCHIP's methodology as a foundation, the USDA and the Census Bureau developed a food security module to be included in the Current Population Survey (CPS).

Since 1995 the U.S. Census Bureau has conducted an annual survey of food security among a nationally representative sample of people living in the United States using the food security module in the CPS. The questions asked are about anxiety that the household budget is inadequate to buy enough food; inadequacy in the quantity or quality of food eaten by adults and children in the household; and instances of reduced food intake or consequences of reduced food intake for adults and for children.

The survey (called the "food security module") is widely regarded as a reliable indicator of household well-being and will serve as the basis for evaluating our nation's progress in reducing food insecurity—one of the Surgeon General's health objectives for the nation for the year 2010. The goal is to increase food security from 88 percent of all U.S. households (1995) to 94 percent.

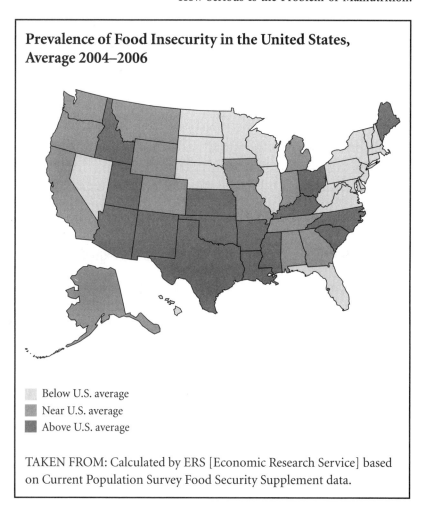

Prevalence of Food Insecurity in the United States, Average 2004–2006

Below U.S. average
Near U.S. average
Above U.S. average

TAKEN FROM: Calculated by ERS [Economic Research Service] based on Current Population Survey Food Security Supplement data.

Revising the Methodology

In 2006, the USDA Economic Research Service asked the National Academies of Science to carry out an independent review of the survey methodology. They concluded that the survey and the methodology to measure food insecurity were appropriate and that it was important to continue monitoring food security. However, they felt that the descriptions of categories should be revised to better convey that it is a measure of household food insecurity.

As a result of the scientific panel's review and subsequent recommendations, USDA introduced new labels for the survey results. These are intended to measure the full range of food insecurity as experienced by households. While the word hunger has been removed from the description of the results of the survey, it should *not* be interpreted that there has been a major shift in the incidence of hunger. There are countless people in this country facing hunger daily.

The new terms used in the survey to describe *food security* are:

- *High Food Security:* These are households that did not answer 'yes' to any of the food insecurity questions.

- *Marginal Food Security:* This term captures families that answered 'yes' to one or two of the food security questions, meaning they have had some difficulties with securing enough food. Previously, they would have been categorized as "Food Secure."

These two groups together will describe *food insecurity*. The new terms used in the survey are:

- *Low Food Security:* This term replaces "Food Insecurity without Hunger." Generally, people that fall into this category have had to make changes in the quality or the quantity of their food in order to deal with a limited budget.

- *Very Low Food Security:* This term replaces "Food Insecurity with Hunger." People that fall into this category have struggled with having enough food for the household, including cutting back or skipping meals on a frequent basis for both adults and children.

According to the results of the Census Bureau survey, those at greatest risk of being hungry or on the edge of hunger (i.e., food insecure) live in households that are: headed by a single woman; Hispanic or Black; or with incomes below the poverty line. Overall, households with children experience food insecurity at almost double the rate for households without children. Geographically, food insecurity is more common in central city households. The survey data also show that households are more likely to be hungry or food insecure if they live in states in the Midwest and South.

What Are the Implications of High Hunger Rates?

The ability to obtain enough food for an active, healthy life is the most basic of human needs. Food insecure households cannot achieve this fundamental element of well-being. They are the ones in our country most likely to be hungry, undernourished, and in poor health, and the ones most in need of assistance. A high number of food insecure households in a nation with our economic plenty means that the fruits of our economy, and the benefits of public and private programs for needy people, are not yet reaching millions of low-income people who are at great risk.

> "There is little or no evidence of poverty-induced malnutrition in the United States."

Malnutrition Is Not a Severe Problem in the United States

Robert E. Rector and Kirk A. Johnson

Robert E. Rector is a Heritage Foundation senior research fellow and has written extensively on the subject of poverty in the United States. Kirk A. Johnson is currently a visiting fellow at the Heritage Foundation, and was previously a senior policy analyst in the Heritage Foundation's Center for Data Analysis, where he conducted quantitative analyses of a broad range of social and economic topics. In the following viewpoint, they argue that America's poor do not suffer from malnutrition, and in fact, are generally well-nourished.

As you read, consider the following questions:

1. How many Americans were living in poverty in 2003, according to U.S. Census Bureau statistics?
2. How does a poor child's average consumption of protein, vitamins, and minerals compare to that of a middle-class child?

Robert E. Rector and Kirk A. Johnson, "Understanding Poverty in America," *The Heritage Foundation*, Backgrounder #1713, January 5, 2004. Reproduced by permission.

3. Are the poor more likely to eat low-nutrient and high-fat diets than the middle class, according to the viewpoint?

Poverty is an important and emotional issue. Last year [2003], the Census Bureau released its annual report on poverty in the United States declaring that there were nearly 35 million poor persons living in this country in 2002, a small increase from the preceding year. To understand poverty in America, it is important to look behind these numbers—to look at the actual living conditions of the individuals the government deems to be poor.

For most Americans, the word "poverty" suggests destitution: an inability to provide a family with nutritious food, clothing, and reasonable shelter. But only a small number of the 35 million persons classified as "poor" by the Census Bureau fit that description. While real material hardship certainly does occur, it is limited in scope and severity. Most of America's "poor" live in material conditions that would be judged as comfortable or well-off just a few generations ago. Today, the expenditures per person of the lowest-income one-fifth (or quintile) of households equal those of the median American household in the early 1970s, after adjusting for inflation.

The following are facts about persons defined as "poor" by the Census Bureau, taken from various government reports:

- Forty-six percent of all poor households actually own their own homes. The average home owned by persons classified as poor by the Census Bureau is a three-bedroom house with one-and-a-half baths, a garage, and a porch or patio.

- Seventy-six percent of poor households have air conditioning. By contrast, 30 years ago, only 36 percent of the entire U.S. population enjoyed air conditioning.

- Only 6 percent of poor households are overcrowded. More than two-thirds have more than two rooms per person.

- The average poor American has more living space than the average individual living in Paris, London, Vienna, Athens, and other cities throughout Europe. (These comparisons are to the average citizens in foreign countries, not to those classified as poor.)

- Nearly three-quarters of poor households own a car; 30 percent own two or more cars.

- Ninety-seven percent of poor households have a color television; over half own two or more color televisions.

- Seventy-eight percent have a VCR or DVD player; 62 percent have cable or satellite TV reception.

- Seventy-three percent own microwave ovens, more than half have a stereo, and a third have an automatic dishwasher.

As a group, America's poor are far from being chronically undernourished. The average consumption of protein, vitamins, and minerals is virtually the same for poor and middle-class children and, in most cases, is well above recommended norms. Poor children actually consume more meat than do higher-income children and have average protein intakes 100 percent above recommended levels. Most poor children today are, in fact, supernourished and grow up to be, on average, one inch taller and ten pounds heavier than the GIs who stormed the beaches of Normandy in World War II.

While the poor are generally well-nourished, some poor families do experience hunger, meaning a temporary discomfort due to food shortages. According to the U.S. Department of Agriculture (USDA), 13 percent of poor families and 2.6 percent of poor children experience hunger at some point during the year. In most cases, their hunger is short-term.

Eighty-nine percent of the poor report their families have "enough" food to eat, while only 2 percent say they "often" do not have enough to eat.

The Typical American

Overall, the typical American defined as poor by the government has a car, air conditioning, a refrigerator, a stove, a clothes washer and dryer, and a microwave. He has two color televisions, cable or satellite TV reception, a VCR or DVD player, and a stereo. He is able to obtain medical care. His home is in good repair and is not overcrowded. By his own report, his family is not hungry and he had sufficient funds in the past year to meet his family's essential needs. While this individual's life is not opulent, it is equally far from the popular images of dire poverty conveyed by the press, liberal activists, and politicians.

Of course, the living conditions of the average poor American should not be taken as representing all the poor. There is actually a wide range in living conditions among the poor. For example, over a quarter of poor households have cell phones and telephone answering machines, but, at the other extreme, approximately one-tenth have no phone at all. While the majority of poor households do not experience significant material problems, roughly a third do experience at least one problem such as overcrowding, temporary hunger, or difficulty getting medical care.

Major Reasons for Child Poverty in America

The best news is that remaining poverty can readily be reduced further, particularly among children. There are two main reasons that American children are poor: Their parents don't work much, and fathers are absent from the home.

In good economic times or bad, the typical poor family with children is supported by only 800 hours of work during

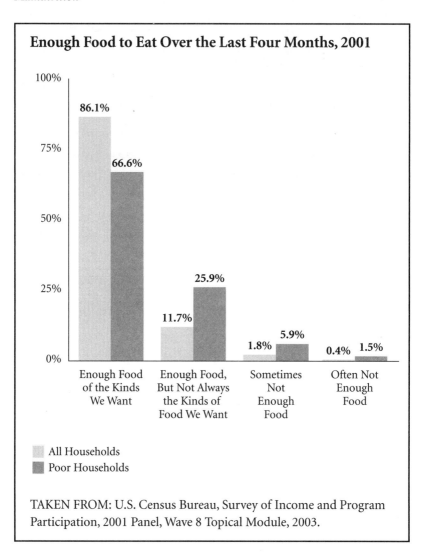

Enough Food to Eat Over the Last Four Months, 2001

All Households
Poor Households

TAKEN FROM: U.S. Census Bureau, Survey of Income and Program Participation, 2001 Panel, Wave 8 Topical Module, 2003.

a year: That amounts to 16 hours of work per week. If work in each family were raised to 2,000 hours per year—the equivalent of one adult working 40 hours per week throughout the year—nearly 75 percent of poor children would be lifted out of official poverty.

Father absence is another major cause of child poverty. Nearly two-thirds of poor children reside in single-parent homes; each year, an additional 1.3 million children are born out of wedlock. If poor mothers married the fathers of their children, almost three-quarters would immediately be lifted out of poverty.

While work and marriage are steady ladders out of poverty, the welfare system perversely remains hostile to both. Major programs such as food stamps, public housing, and Medicaid continue to reward idleness and penalize marriage. If welfare could be turned around to encourage work and marriage, remaining poverty would drop quickly. . . .

Hunger and Malnutrition in America

There are frequent charges of widespread hunger and malnutrition in the United States. To understand these assertions, it is important, first of all, to distinguish between hunger and the more severe problem of malnutrition. Malnutrition (also called undernutrition) is a condition of reduced health due to a chronic shortage of calories and nutriments. There is little or no evidence of poverty-induced malnutrition in the United States.

Hunger is a far less severe condition: a temporary but real discomfort caused by an empty stomach. The government defines hunger as "the uneasy or painful sensation caused by lack of food." While hunger due to a lack of financial resources does occur in the United States, it is limited in scope and duration. According to the USDA [United States Department of Agriculture], on a typical day, fewer than one American in 200 will experience hunger due to a lack of money to buy food. The hunger rate rises somewhat when examined over a longer time period; according to the USDA, some 6.9 million Americans, or 2.4 percent of the population, were hungry at least once during 2002. Nearly all hunger in the United States is short-term and episodic rather than continuous.

Some 92 percent of those who experienced hunger in 2002 were adults, and only 8 percent were children. Overall, some

567,000 children, or 0.8 percent of all children, were hungry at some point in 2002. In a typical month, roughly one child in 400 skipped one or more meals because the family lacked funds to buy food.

Not only is hunger relatively rare among U.S. children, but it has declined sharply since the mid-1990s. [The] number of hungry children was cut by a third between 1995 and 2002. According to the USDA, in 1995, there were 887,000 hungry children: by 2002, the number had fallen to 567,000.

Overall, some 97 percent of the U.S. population lived in families that reported they had "enough food to eat" during the entire year, although not always the kinds of foods they would have preferred. Around 2.5 percent stated their families "sometimes" did not have "enough to eat" due to money shortages, and one-half of 1 percent (0.5 percent) said they "often" did not have enough to eat due to a lack of funds.

Hunger and Poverty

Among the poor, the hunger rate was obviously higher: During 2002, 12.8 percent of the poor lived in households in which at least one member experienced hunger at some point. Among poor children, 2.4 percent experienced hunger at some point in the year. Overall, most poor households were not hungry and did not experience food shortages during the year.

When asked, some 89 percent of poor households reported they had "enough food to eat" during the entire year, although not always the kinds of food they would prefer. Around 9 percent stated they "sometimes" did not have enough to eat because of a lack of money to buy food. Another 2 percent of the poor stated that they "often" did not have enough to eat due to a lack of funds.

Poverty and Malnutrition

It is widely believed that a lack of financial resources forces poor people to eat low-quality diets that are deficient in nutriments and high in fat. However, survey data show that nutriment density (amount of vitamins, minerals, and protein per kilocalorie of food) does not vary by income class. Nor do the poor consume higher-fat diets than do the middle class; the percentage of persons with high fat intake (as a share of total calories) is virtually the same for low-income and upper-middle-income persons. Overconsumption of calories in general, however, is a major problem among the poor, as it is within the general U.S. population.

Examination of the average nutriment consumption of Americans reveals that age and gender play a far greater role than income class in determining nutritional intake. For example, the nutriment intakes of adult women in the upper middle class (with incomes above 350 percent of the poverty level) more closely resemble the intakes of poor women than they do those of upper-middle-class men, children, or teens. The average nutriment consumption of upper-middle-income preschoolers, as a group, is virtually identical with that of poor preschoolers but not with the consumption of adults or older children in the upper middle class.

This same pattern holds for adult males, teens, and most other age and gender groups. In general, children aged 0–11 years have the highest average level of nutriment intakes relative to the recommended daily allowance (RDA), followed by adult and teen males. Adult and teen females have the lowest level of intakes. This pattern holds for all income classes.

Nutrition and Poor Children

Government surveys provide little evidence of widespread undernutrition among poor children; in fact, they show that the average nutriment consumption among the poor closely resembles that of the upper middle class. For example, children in families with incomes below the poverty level actually consume more meat than do children in families with incomes at

350 percent of the poverty level or higher (roughly $65,000 for a family of four in today's [2004] dollars). . . .

The intake of nutriments is very similar for poor and middle-class children and is generally well above the recommended daily level. For example, the consumption of protein (a relatively expensive nutriment) among poor children is, on average, between 150 percent and 267 percent of the RDA.

When shortfalls of specific vitamins and minerals appear (for example, among teenage girls), they tend to be very similar for the poor and the middle class. While poor teenage girls, on average, tend to underconsume vitamin E, vitamin B-6, calcium, phosphorus, magnesium, iron, and zinc, a virtually identical underconsumption of these same nutriments appears among upper-middle-class girls.

> *"The public health impact is enormous: More than half of the world's disease burden—measured in 'years of healthy life lost'—is attributable to hunger, overeating, and widespread vitamin and mineral deficiencies."*

Obesity and Malnutrition Are Related and Both Are Severe Problems

The Sustainability Report

The Sustainability Report is a Canadian, Internet-based report-ing organization that provides independent reporting on issues regarding more sustainable forms of development. In the follow-ing viewpoint, the organization notes that both the obese and the underfed can suffer from malnutrition, outlines the consequences of the growing problem of obesity on governments and health systems, and proposes several steps to alleviate malnutrition and obesity.

As you read, consider the following questions:

1. According to statistics, how many overweight people are there in the world as of 2004?

The Sustainability Report, "Chronic Hunger and Obesity Epidemic Eroding Global Progress," 2004. Reproduced by permission.

2. What are the consequences of underconsumption and overconsumption on adults and children, according to the authors?

3. In the late 1990s, how much money did the United States spend on fighting obesity, according to *The Sustainability Report?*

For the first time in human history, the number of overweight people rivals the number of underweight people, according to a new report [2004] from the Worldwatch Institute, a Washington, DC-based research organization. While the world's underfed population has declined slightly since 1980 to 1.2 billion, the number of overweight people has surged to 1.2 billion.

Both the overweight and the underweight suffer from malnutrition, a deficiency or an excess in a person's intake of nutrients and other dietary elements needed for healthy living. "The hungry and the overweight share high levels of sickness and disability, shortened life expectancies, and lower levels of productivity—each of which is a drag on a country's development," said Gary Gardner, co-author with Brian Halweil of *Underfed and Overfed: The Global Epidemic of Malnutrition.* The public health impact is enormous: More than half of the world's disease burden—measured in "years of healthy life lost"—is attributable to hunger, overeating, and widespread vitamin and mineral deficiencies.

"The century with the greatest potential to eliminate malnutrition instead saw it boosted to record levels," said Gardner.

The number of hungry people remains high in a world of food surpluses. In the developing world, there are 150 million underweight children, nearly one in three. And in Africa, both the share and the absolute number of children who are underweight are on the rise.

Meanwhile, the population of overweight people has expanded rapidly in recent decades, more than offsetting the health gains from the modest decline in hunger. In the United States, 55 percent of adults are overweight by international standards. A whopping 23 percent of American adults are considered obese. And the trend is spreading to children as well, with one in five American kids now classified as overweight.

Consequences of Hunger and Obesity

The specific consequences of hunger and being overweight can be very different. Hunger hits children the hardest, increasing their vulnerability to infectious diseases or conditions such as diarrhea, which often lead to permanent mental and physical impairment or even death. Excess weight gain, on the other hand, takes its greatest toll in adulthood, leading to chronic, but reversible, conditions such as heart disease and diabetes.

Both developed and developing nations are paying a high price for malnutrition. The World Bank estimates that hunger cost India between 3 and 9 percent of its GDP [Gross Domestic Product] in 1996. And obesity cost the United States 12 percent of the national health care budget in the late 1990s, $118 billion, more than double the $47 billion attributable to smoking.

Surprisingly, overweight and obesity are advancing rapidly in the developing world as well. "Often, nations have simply traded hunger for obesity, and diseases of poverty for diseases of excess," said co-author Brian Halweil. In Brazil and Colombia, for example, 36 and 41 percent, respectively, of the population is overweight, levels that match those of many European countries. Still struggling to eradicate infectious diseases, many developing nations' health care systems could be crippled by growing caseloads of chronic illness.

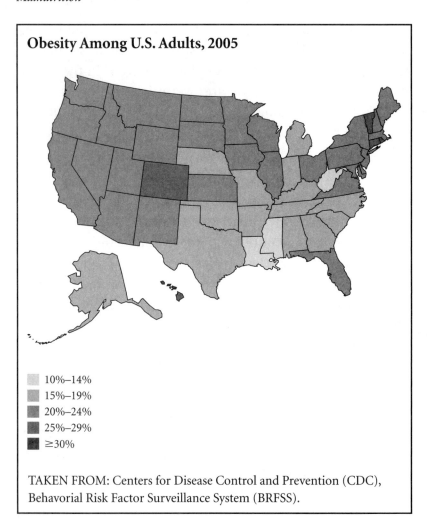

Obesity Among U.S. Adults, 2005

10%–14%
15%–19%
20%–24%
25%–29%
≥30%

TAKEN FROM: Centers for Disease Control and Prevention (CDC), Behavorial Risk Factor Surveillance System (BRFSS).

"While the myth persists that hunger results from a scarcity of food, inequitable distribution of resources and gender discrimination prevent most of the world's hungry from getting enough to eat," said Halweil. Some 80 percent of the world's hungry children live in countries with food surpluses, for example. The common thread that runs through nearly all hunger, in rich and poor nations alike, is poverty.

Since women, as farmers and mothers, are nutritional gatekeepers in many countries, boosting their status is a big step toward improving national nutrition. A 1999 analysis of malnutrition in 63 nations found that improvements in women's education, access to health care, and living environment were responsible for 75 percent of the reductions in underweight among children.

And eliminating micronutrient deficiencies can produce rapid results for just pennies per person per year. The World Health Organization [WHO] program to iodize salt in 47 countries between 1994 and 1997 cut the prevalence of iodine deficiency disorder from 29 percent to 13 percent.

Making Nutrition a Priority

Most countries simply do not make nutritional well-being a priority. But even countries struggling with difficult economic and political circumstances can significantly reduce the number of underweight people with the right policies. Cuba and the Indian state of Kerala, for example, have been remarkably successful at reducing malnutrition by targeting nutritionally vulnerable populations such as women and children for special attention. Both governments provide broad access to health care, an important partner to food intake in ensuring good nutrition.

In nations where overeating is a problem, policy makers need a different set of tools. All too often, technofixes like liposuction or olestra attract more attention than the behavioral patterns like poor eating habits and sedentary lifestyles that underlie obesity. Liposuction is now the leading form of cosmetic surgery in the United States, for example, at 400,000 operations per year. While billions are spent on gimmicky diets and food advertising, far too little money is spent on nutrition education.

"In the absence of a strong government educational effort on nutrition issues—in schools, on product labels, and through the regulation of food advertising—most people get their nutrition cues from food companies," said Gardner.

"In the modern food environment, we're like children in a candy shop, every day of our lives."

Starting Nutritional Literacy Early

Improving nutritional literacy can begin in schools. In Singapore, the Trim and Fit Scheme has reduced obesity among children by 33 to 50 percent, depending on the age group, through changes in school catering and increased nutrition and physical education for teachers and children. School cafeterias in Berkeley, California, have gone organic, with some of the produce for meals coming from student-tended gardens on campus.

A serious effort to end overeating could be modeled on the successful campaign to discourage smoking, including the use of "high fat" or "high sodium" warning labels and taxes to deter purchases. Consumption of nutrient-poor foods could be further reduced using a tax on food based on the nutrient value per calorie, as advocated by Yale psychologist Kelly Brownell. Fatty and sugary foods low in nutrients and high in calories would be taxed the most, while fruits and vegetables might escape taxation entirely.

> *"The United Nations these days possesses two left thumbs, most concretely when it addresses nutrition. . . . And even as WHO [World Health Organization] bureaucrats furiously add and subtract calories, millions of third worlders succumb to diseases that industrialized nations vanquished decades ago."*

Undernutrition Is a More Serious Problem than Obesity

Deroy Murdock

Deroy Murdock is a political analyst, syndicated newspaper columnist, and contributing writer for the National Review. *He is also a media fellow with the Hoover Institute at Stanford University and a senior fellow at the Atlas Economic Research Foundation. In the following viewpoint, Murdock asserts that the World Health Organization's recent emphasis on eradicating "globesity" is coming at the expense of the more serious problems—malnutrition and diseases such as malaria, measles, and tuberculosis.*

Deroy Murdock, "Nutritional Schizophrenia," *National Review Online*, June 25, 2002. Reproduced by permission.

Malnutrition

As you read, consider the following questions:

1. According to the World Health Organization (WHO), how many children under the age of five worldwide are overweight or obese?
2. What percentage of deaths of children under age five were associated with undernutrition in 1999, according to the WHO?
3. How many children die between birth and five years old worldwide from various ailments "often in combination with malnutrition"?

President [Ronald] Reagan once quipped that sometimes in his administration, "the right hand doesn't know what the far-right hand is doing." The United Nations [UN] these days possesses two left thumbs, most concretely when it addresses nutrition. The UN's World Health Organization [WHO] strives both to shrink *and* expand waistlines across the globe. And even as WHO bureaucrats furiously add and subtract calories, millions of third worlders succumb to diseases that industrialized nations vanquished decades ago.

WHO wants to drive obesity from Earth. In a recent draft document, the agency advocated taxes and marketing restrictions on sugar-rich foods to stamp out "globesity." WHO also claims that worldwide, 22 million children under age five are overweight or obese.

But its own Web site shows that WHO believes children are too thin as well as too fat.

Fully 60 percent of all deaths of children under age five were associated with undernutrition in 1999, WHO reports. An online report on infectious disease explains that various ailments "often in combination with malnutrition" annually kill five million kids between birth and five years. Jacques Diouf, director of the UN Food and Agriculture Organization, wisely reminded the *New York Times* that around the world, "There are still 80 million people who don't have enough money to buy the food they need."

WHO staffers who worry about hunger have it right. True, millions suffer from obesity in the industrial West, especially here [in the United States]. After spending 10 days among the svelte citizens of Hong Kong, Beijing, and Tokyo in 1995, for example, I flew 14 hours nonstop from Narita Airport, outside Japan's capital, to Newark. The first Americans I saw upon deplaning were a pair of U.S. Customs officers. They must have weighed 250 pounds each. Their thighs cascaded over the stools they occupied. "Home at last," I thought to myself.

Obesity a Disease of Individual Choice

But Americans and Europeans (who tend to be thinner than us anyway) have access to Slimfast and Stairmaster. Switching from fat-drenched meals to sea kelp and seltzer—and plenty in-between—is a matter of individual choice, responsibility, and willpower in the G-8 countries. Westerners have as many options as notches in their belts.

Too many in the third world wonder, though, when they might eat again. Even worse, if that is possible, are the myriad exotic diseases that still wipe them out. The WHO's African region endures a staggering mortality rate of 163 deaths per 1,000 live births among children under age five (versus 101 in the Eastern Mediterranean and 30 in the Americas' regions).

In 2000, malaria killed 906,000 children, mainly in sub-Saharan Africa. Picture 34 loaded school buses plunging fatally over a cliff every day. Measles kills nearly 1 million kids per year, 450,000 of them African. Tuberculosis takes 1.7 million lives each year, primarily among adolescents and adults. Meanwhile, diarrhea-related ailments killed 2.2 million people in 1998.

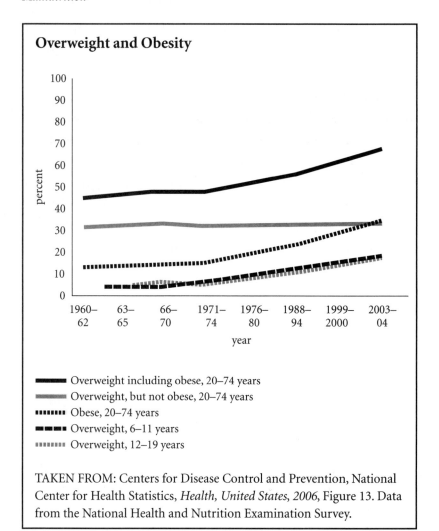

Overweight and Obesity

Overweight including obese, 20–74 years
Overweight, but not obese, 20–74 years
Obese, 20–74 years
Overweight, 6–11 years
Overweight, 12–19 years

TAKEN FROM: Centers for Disease Control and Prevention, National Center for Health Statistics, *Health, United States, 2006*, Figure 13. Data from the National Health and Nutrition Examination Survey.

WHO Has Priorities Wrong

Rather than fret over rotund capitalists who can fend for themselves, WHOniks should target their $2.2 billion budget (including at least $185.4 million in U.S. government contributions for 2002-2003) against the third world's deadly microbes and the parasites that transmit them. WHO luminaries should heed Treasury Secretary Paul O'Neill. While in Africa last month with U2's lead singer, Bono, O'Neill found a water-purification plant that was completed in exchange for $2,000 in debt forgiveness. As columnist Philip Terzian notes, O'Neill calculated that Uganda could spend $2,000-per-well and offer its citizens clean water for a total of $25 million.

Basic sanitation and vaccines would help enormously. Likewise, allowing African villagers to spray DDT inside their homes would shield them from malarial mosquitoes. Instead, Western aid agencies fight DDT because of the risks it once posed to America's most majestic birds. The trouble, of course, is that Africa is short on bald eagles and long on dead babies.

The UN's nutritional schizophrenia erupted in Rome, as the *Times* of London reports. Delegates to the UN's World Food Summit, mainly from the third world, arrived at the June 10 kickoff luncheon in police-escorted limousines. Some 170 waiters served the 3,000 global menu cops foie gras, lobster vinaigrette, filet of goose stuffed with olives and fruit compote to close. No doubt, they dreamed of Americans dining on salad and iced tea.

Periodical Bibliography

The following articles have been selected to supplement the diverse views presented in this chapter.

Ronald Bailey   "Counterterrorism, Conflict Prevention, or Hunger: Which Would You Spend Money On?" *Reason Magazine*, May 27, 2008.

Dorothy Carey   "Soaring Food Prices—'A Global Crisis,'" *Nutridate*, July 2008.

Scott Elder   "The Hungry Planet," *National Geographic*, June 2006.

Michael Learner   "Responding to the Global Hunger Crisis," *Bread for the World*, June 2008.

Samuel Loewenberg   "Starving Season," *Salon*, June 13, 2006.

Fred Magdoff   "A Precarious Existence: The Fate of Billions?" *Monthly Review*, February 2004.

Anna Quindlen   "Obesity More Prevalent Than Hunger," *Future Survey*, December 2007."Real Food for Thought," *Newsweek*, December 11, 2006.

John Rennie   "All You Can't Eat," *Scientific American*, September 2007.

Jonathan Schwarz   "Charity Begins at Home," *Mother Jones*, September-October 2007.

Aliya Sternstein   "The Starvelings," *Economist*, January 26, 2008.

"Sharper Pangs of Food Insecurity," *CQ Weekly*, May 12, 2008.

Gary Stix   "A Question of Sustenance," *Scientific American*, September 2007.

Michael Wines   "Malnutrition Is Cheating Its Survivors, and Africa's Future," *New York Times*, December 28, 2006.

OPPOSING VIEWPOINTS® SERIES

CHAPTER 2

What Are the Root Causes of Malnutrition?

Chapter Preface

Malnutrition is a condition caused by a lack of food and/or proper nutrients that can result in serious health and cognitive problems—and even death. In most cases, it is directly related to hunger: If persons are not getting adequate amounts of food on a regular basis, they will suffer from malnutrition because they are not getting the nutrients their bodies need to grow and remain healthy. Yet according to the Food and Agriculture Organization of the United Nations (FAO), there is enough food to provide everyone in the world with at least 2,720 kilocalories (kcal) per person per day. So why are hunger and malnutrition still serious problems in the twenty-first century?

It is vital to determine the causes of malnutrition because this is the only way to comprehensively address the problem. Some of the major causes of malnutrition seem obvious. Poverty, for example, is a clear cause of hunger and malnutrition. If a family does not have the financial resources to purchase the right kinds of food on a regular basis, chances are that they are at a high risk for malnutrition. War is another obvious cause, as conflict can cause widespread destruction of crops and cattle, displacement, and poverty. Famine, which is defined as an extreme shortage of food, can also result in malnutrition in underdeveloped areas. Other obvious root causes are poor sanitation and dirty water, which cause diarrhea, resulting in a loss of nutrients and other illnesses.

Some root causes of malnutrition are not so obvious. Aging, for example, is one that does not quickly come to mind for most people. Yet studies show that the elderly suffer from a surprisingly high rate of malnutrition for a number of physiological, psychological, and economic reasons. Gender inequality is also considered to bring about malnutrition. Without access to education and resources, women are at a severe disadvantage when it comes to providing for their families and themselves.

In recent years, new causes of malnutrition have emerged. Biofuels, particularly the popularity of ethanol, have become a contentious issue in the malnutrition debate. Some critics contend that biofuels, made from corn or other common agricultural crops, will take away much-needed land and other resources for food production and raise food prices significantly. Global warming is another controversial issue related to malnutrition. While some commentators argue that climate change has increased crop failures and loss of fish and livestock, others contend that bad government is at fault, not the environment.

In the debate about malnutrition and why it is still such a major problem in the twenty-first century, some of the reasons are clear cut, while others remain contentious. The viewpoints in this chapter explore the root causes of malnutrition as well as the controversies surrounding them.

> *"The causes of poverty include poor people's lack of resources, an extremely unequal income distribution in the world and within specific countries, conflict, and hunger itself."*

Poverty Is a Root Cause of Malnutrition

World Hunger Notes

World Hunger Notes is an online publication of the World Hunger Education Service, an organization that works to inform policy makers and the public about the causes, extent, and efforts to eradicate poverty and hunger in the United States and the rest of the world. In the following viewpoint, the organization contends that poverty is a principal cause of hunger and widespread malnutrition. The viewpoint also discusses the root causes of poverty in the developing world.

As you read, consider the following questions:

1. According to the United Nations Food and Agriculture Organization, how many people in the world suffered from malnutrition in 2006?

World Hunger Notes, "World Hunger Facts 2008," March 1, 2008. Reproduced by permission.

2. Geographically, what percentage of malnourished children lives in Asia, Africa, and South America and the Caribbean?

3. How many people in the world live on one dollar a day or less, according to 2004 statistics published by the World Bank?

Hunger is a term which has three meanings

- the uneasy or painful sensation caused by want of food; craving appetite. Also the exhausted condition caused by want of food

- the want or scarcity of food in a country

- a strong desire or craving

World hunger refers to the second definition, aggregated to the world level. The related technical term (in this case operationalized in medicine) is malnutrition.

Malnutrition is a general term that indicates a lack of some or all nutritional elements necessary for human health.

There are two basic types of malnutrition. The first and most important is protein-energy malnutrition—the lack of enough protein (from meat and other sources) and food that provides energy (measured in calories) which all of the basic food groups provide. This is the type of malnutrition that is referred to when world hunger is discussed. The second type of malnutrition, also very important, is micronutrient (vitamin and mineral) deficiency. This is not the type of malnutrition that is referred to when world hunger is discussed, though it is certainly very important.

[Recently there has also been a move to include obesity as a third form of malnutrition. Considering obesity as malnutrition expands the previous usual meaning of the term, which referred to poor nutrition due to lack of food inputs. It is poor nutrition, but it is certainly not typically due to a lack of calories, but rather too many (although poor food choices, often due to poverty, are part of the problem). Obesity will not be considered here, although obesity is certainly a health problem and is increasingly considered as a type of malnutrition.]

Protein-energy Malnutrition

Protein-energy malnutrition (PEM) is the most lethal form of malnutrition/hunger. It is basically a lack of calories and protein. Food is converted into energy by humans, and the energy contained in food is measured by calories. Protein is necessary for key body functions including provision of essential amino acids and development and maintenance of muscles.

No one really knows how many people are malnourished. The statistic most frequently cited is that of the United Nations Food and Agriculture Organization [FAO], which measures 'undernutrition.' The most recent estimate (2006) of the FAO says that 854 million people worldwide are undernourished. This is 12.6 percent of the estimated world population of 6.6 billion. Most of the undernourished—820 million—are in developing countries. The FAO estimate is based on statistical aggregates. It looks at a country's income level and income distribution and uses this information to estimate how many people receive such a low level of income that they are malnourished. It is not an estimate based on seeing to what extent actual people are malnourished and projecting from there (as would be done by survey sampling). [It has been argued that the FAO approach is not sufficient to give accurate estimates of malnutrition.]

Undernutrition is a relatively new concept, but is increasingly used. It should be taken as basically equivalent to malnutrition. (It should be said as an aside, that the idea of undernourishment, its relationship to malnutrition, and the reasons for its emergence as a concept is not clear to *Hunger Notes*.)

Children Are Most Visible Victims

Children are the most visible victims of undernutrition. Children who are poorly nourished suffer up to 160 days of illness each year. Poor nutrition plays a role in at least half of the 10.9 million child deaths each year—five million deaths. Undernutrition magnifies the effect of every disease, including measles and malaria. The estimated proportions of deaths in which undernutrition is an underlying cause are roughly similar for diarrhea (61 percent), malaria (57 percent), pneumonia (52 percent), and measles (45 percent). Malnutrition can also be caused by diseases, such as the diseases that cause diarrhea, by reducing the body's ability to convert food into usable nutrients.

According to the most recent estimate that *Hunger Notes* could find, malnutrition, as measured by stunting, affects 32.5 percent of children in developing countries—one of three. Geographically, more than 70 percent of malnourished children live in Asia, 26 percent in Africa and 4 percent in Latin America and the Caribbean. In many cases, their plight began even before birth with a malnourished mother. Undernutrition among pregnant women in developing countries leads to 1 out of 6 infants born with low birth weight. This is not only a risk factor for neonatal deaths, but also causes learning disabilities, mental retardation, poor health, blindness and premature death.

The world produces enough food to feed everyone. World agriculture produces 17 percent more calories per person today than it did 30 years ago, despite a 70 percent population increase. This is enough to provide everyone in the world with at least 2,720 kilocalories (kcal) per person per day. The prin-

Living on $1 a Day

Region	% in $1 a day poverty	Population (millions)	Pop. in $1 a day poverty (millions)
East Asia and Pacific	9.07	1,885.0	170.0
Latin America and the Caribbean	8.63	549.0	47.0
South Asia	31.08	1,470.0	456.0
Sub-Saharan Africa	41.09	753.0	309.0
Total developing countries			**982.0**
Europe and Central Asia	0.95	460.0	1.0
Middle East and North Africa	1.47	306.0	4.0
Total			987

TAKEN FROM: World Hunger Education Service, "World Hunger Facts 2008," *Hunger Notes*, March 1, 2008. www.worldhunger.org.

cipal problem is that many people in the world do not have sufficient land to grow, or income to purchase, enough food.

Poverty is the principal cause of hunger. The causes of poverty include poor people's lack of resources, an extremely unequal income distribution in the world and within specific countries, conflict, and hunger itself. As of 2008 (2004 statistics), the World Bank has estimated that there were an estimated 982 million poor people in developing countries who live on $1 a day or less. This compares to the FAO estimate of 850 million undernourished people. Extreme poverty remains an alarming problem in the world's developing regions, despite the advances made in the 1990s till now, which reduced "dollar a day" poverty from (an estimated) 1.23 billion people to 982 million in 2004, a reduction of 20 percent over the period. Progress in poverty reduction has been concentrated in Asia, and especially, East Asia, with the major improvement occurring in China. In Sub-Saharan Africa, the number of people in extreme poverty has increased.

Conflict as a cause of hunger and poverty. The United Nations High Commissioner for Refugees (UNHCR) reports that as of December 2006, there were at least 22.7 million displaced, including 9.9 million refugees and 12.8 million internally displaced persons. (Refugees flee to another country while internally displaced people move to another area or their own country.) Most people become refugees or are internally displaced as a result of conflict, though there are also natural causes such as drought, earthquakes, and flooding. In the early stages of refugee emergencies, malnutrition runs rampant, exponentially increasing the risk of disease and death. But, important and (relatively) visible though it is, conflict is less important as poverty as a cause of hunger. (Using the statistics above 798 million people suffer from chronic hunger while 22.7 million people are displaced.)

Hunger is also a cause of poverty. By causing poor health, low levels of energy, and even mental impairment, hunger can lead to even greater poverty by reducing people's ability to work and learn.

Progress Is Slow

Progress in reducing the number of hungry people. The target set at the 1996 World Food Summit was to halve the number of undernourished people by 2015 from their number in 1990–92. (FAO uses three year averages in its calculation of undernourished people.) The (estimated) number of undernourished people in developing countries was 824 million in 1990–92. In 2000–02, the number had declined only slightly to 820 million (854 million worldwide including countries in transition—formerly part of the Soviet bloc—and developed countries.)

So, overall, the world is not making progress toward the world food summit goal, although there has been progress in Asia, and Latin America and the Caribbean.

Micronutrients

Micronutrients. Quite a few trace elements or micronutrients—vitamins and minerals—are important for health. One out of 3 people in developing countries are affected by vitamin and mineral deficiencies, according to the World Health Organization. Three—perhaps the most important in terms of current health consequences for poor people in developing countries—are:

Vitamin A. Vitamin A deficiency can cause night blindness and reduces the body's resistance to disease. In children, Vitamin A deficiency can also cause growth retardation. Between 100 and 140 million children are vitamin A deficient. An estimated 250,000 to 500,000 vitamin A-deficient children become blind every year, half of them dying within 12 months of losing their sight.

Iron. Iron deficiency is a principal cause of anemia. Two billion people—over 30 percent of the world's population—are anemic, mainly due to iron deficiency, and, in developing countries, frequently exacerbated by malaria and worm infections. For children, health consequences include premature birth, low birth weight, infections, and elevated risk of death. Later, physical and cognitive development are impaired, resulting in lowered school performance. For pregnant women, anemia contributes to 20 percent of all maternal deaths.

Iodine. Iodine deficiency disorders (IDD) jeopardize children's mental health—often their very lives. Serious iodine deficiency during pregnancy may result in stillbirths, abortions and congenital abnormalities such as cretinism, a grave, irreversible form of mental retardation that affects people living in iodine-deficient areas of Africa and Asia. IDD also causes mental impairment that lowers intellectual prowess at home, at school, and at work. IDD affects over 740 million people, 13 percent of the world's population. Fifty million people have some degree of mental impairment caused by IDD.

"*Famine is a complex process, not a unique, abrupt event. Food prices escalate, families sell their property, some of them migrate. As hunger grows, health systems collapse, the physical condition of individuals declines and people begin to die from malnutrition and illness.*"

Conflict and Food Politicization Can Cause Malnutrition

Miren Gutierrez

Miren Gutierrez is the editor-in-chief of the Inter Press Service News Agency, a daily news service that reports on issues that affect third world nations, particularly economics, trade, development, the environment, human rights, and civil society. In the following viewpoint, Gutierrez notes that there is an abundance of food in the world, but that a number of factors prevent the fair distribution of food to all people. She asserts that conflict and food politicization cause some of the worst hunger emergencies, and provides examples of recent food crises in Africa to illustrate the extent of the problem.

Miren Gutierrez, "A World Addicted to Hunger: Part 1," *Global Policy Forum*, May 3, 2006. Reproduced by permission.

As you read, consider the following questions:

1. According to Oxfam International, how many people in the world suffer from chronic hunger?

2. What percentage of food emergencies around the world are caused by man-made disasters, according to the World Food Programme?

3. How have Zimbabwe president Robert Mugabe's government policies and the conflict in the region affected food production?

In a report on Ethiopia issued on February 24 [2006] the Food and Agriculture Organisation (FAO) says that "about 15 million people are facing food insecurity that is either chronic or transitory in nature." Of these, 5 to 6 million people are chronically food insecure (that is, "people who have lost the capacity to produce or buy enough to meet their annual food needs even under normal weather and market conditions"), and the remaining 10 million are vulnerable, "with a weak resilience to any shock," says FAO.

According to Oxfam International, a confederation of anti-poverty organisations, more than 850 million people suffer from chronic hunger. Is Ethiopia condemned to suffer hunger regularly? Are others? "Abundance, not scarcity, best describes the world's food supply," said a 1998 paper entitled "12 Myths About Hunger," published by the Institute for Food and Development Policy/Food First, a U.S.-based nongovernmental organisation. "Even most 'hungry countries' have enough food for all their people right now. Many are net exporters of food and other agricultural products."

The Contradictions of Hunger

One could talk about the contradictions of hunger. For example, in Nigeria, Brazil or Bolivia, abundant food resources coexist with pockets of famine; while Costa Rica has only half the farmed hectares per person that Honduras has, Costa Ricans enjoy a life expectancy 11 years longer than that of Hondurans.

In Ethiopia, the 2005 harvest of cereal and pulse crops—which include peas and beans—was estimated by United Nations agencies FAO and the World Food Programme (WFP) as "very good," and in 2006 the country has a small exportable surplus. "Despite this positive overall situation, large numbers of people, mainly pastoralists in south-eastern Ethiopia, are facing pre-famine conditions due to the failure of seasonal rains," said a group of FAO experts in an e-mail interview.

Similarly, another report published by FAO last December [2005] said that South Africa has harvested a record maize crop of 12.4 million tonnes. However, FAO added: "food insecurity in southern Africa is of serious concern . . . Nearly 12 million people, mainly in Zimbabwe and Malawi, are in need of emergency food assistance."

According to FAO, the surplus of maize in the Republic of South Africa, at more than 4 million tonnes, is more than enough to meet the deficit of the rest of the countries in the region. So why do people die of malnutrition and hunger?

The Malthusian nightmares of geometric population growth combined with an exhaustion of supplies have not materialised. The world's population has arrived at 6.4 billion, six times higher than when Thomas Malthus published his "Essay on the Principle of Population" in 1798. But Malthus had underestimated the human ability to exploit resources increasingly efficiently.

Inequality a Cause of Famine

What humanity does not do so well is to be fair with one another: Most of the specialists and organisations dedicated to fighting against hunger, no matter how different their approach, point at inequality as the main underlying cause. Amartya Sen, Nobel laureate in economics, argued that the

Twenty Years of War in Northern Uganda

For twenty years, northern Uganda has been trapped in a deadly and horrific conflict between the government and the Lords Resistance Army. The conflict has displaced 1.8 million people. Seventy-eight percent of these households have no access to land, 84 percent are dependent upon food relief, with almost 900 excess deaths a week. This situation has caused high levels of chronic malnutrition: for example, about 48 percent of children in Kitgum district are stunted. The economic cost of the war to the region is around $864 million—largely lost agricultural production and labour productivity.

Civil Society Organisation for Peace in Northern Uganda (CSOPNU), "Counting the Cost: Twenty Years of War in Northern Uganda," Causing Hunger an Overview of the Food Crisis in Africa, *p. 22, July 2006. www.oxfam.org.*

lack of entitlement, rather than the lack of available food, is the principal cause of famine in poor countries.

According to Food First as well, famines are the result of "underlying inequities that deprive people, especially poor women, of economic opportunity and security . . . Rapid population growth and hunger are endemic to societies where land ownership, jobs, education, health care, and old age security are beyond the reach of most people." FAO says that "this is a question of unequal distribution, poverty and limited physical and economic access to food by large segments of the population."

Man-Made Disasters a Cause of Famine

Man-made disasters play an increasingly important role. According to WFP, "since 1992, the proportion of short- and long-term food crises that can be attributed to human causes has more than doubled, rising from 15 percent to more than 35 percent."

Conflict a Cause of Famine

Fighting displaces millions of people from their homes, leading to some of the world's worst hunger emergencies, says WFP in a report available on its Web site. In war, food sometimes becomes a weapon: Soldiers will starve opponents by seizing food and livestock. Fields and water wells are often contaminated or destroyed in war, forcing farmers to abandon their land. Famine is a complex process, not a unique, abrupt event. Food prices escalate, families sell their property, some of them migrate. As hunger grows, health systems collapse, the physical condition of individuals declines and people begin to die from malnutrition and illness.

Look at what is happening in Ethiopia. In spite of the advantages for crop-producing families, high cereal prices "will negatively affect the poorer households that are net buyers of grain," says FAO. As a consequence, "a significant number of vulnerable households remain largely food insecure and will depend on humanitarian assistance in 2006." Asked about how the food crisis in the Horn of Africa compares with the situation in Zimbabwe, FAO replied that, "although this is not the only food crisis in Africa, it could be said that (the situation in the Horn of Africa) is currently the most dramatic due to the number of people affected and to their difficult food situation." The crisis in Zimbabwe is more complicated, however. "Total cereal production has steadily fallen from over 3 million tonnes in 1996 to about 800,000 tonnes in 2005. This is a structural decline coinciding with the ongoing land tenure changes and the overall economic deterioration in that country."

President Robert Mugabe has given much of Zimbabwe's farmland to cronies not interested in farming; his policies have ruined the economy and left it short of diesel fuel to run its tractors. Inflation edged over 900 percent in March [2006]. The food crisis in southern Africa is occurring in the middle of the world's worst AIDS epidemic. Without sufficient food, those infected with HIV generally develop AIDS more rapidly and die. "The greatest humanitarian crisis today is not in Pakistan, the tsunami region or Darfur, though they are all severe," said James Morris, executive director of WFP, last October [2005]. "It is the gradual disintegration of social structures in southern Africa."

The immediate cause of famine is widespread crop failure, resulting from drought or civil war. "But not every drought or crop failure has to lead to famine. Countries that are well prepared to handle the crisis manage to protect their vulnerable populations," says FAO. The FAO experts reference Amartya Sen's work: "Democratic societies usually fare better in mitigating the food insecurity crisis and avoiding hardships to its population. One needs to highlight the importance of communication and the fact that often the risk of famine occurs because there is insufficient response to the early warning provided."

"Study after study confirms what should be obvious: Guaranteeing women's human rights is crucial for development and a pathway to economic prosperity."

Gender Inequality Contributes to the Problem of Malnutrition

International Food Policy Research Institute

The International Food Policy Research Institute (IFPRI) is a nongovernmental organization that works for sustainable solutions for ending hunger and poverty. In the following viewpoint, IFPRI claims that women are the key to food security in developing countries. The viewpoint also elucidates the benefits of empowering women through educational and economic opportunities.

As you read, consider the following questions:

1. According to Armartya Sen, how many "missing women" are there in the world?
2. What is the link between women's status and children's nutrition, according to experts?

International Food Policy Research Institute, "The High Price of Gender Inequality," *IFPRI Perspectives*, April 2002. Reproduced by permission of the International Food Policy Research Institute www.ifpri.org.

3. What effect does increasing a female farmer's education have on yields, according to a study by IFPRI researcher Agnes Quisimbing?

If the Taliban had been looking for a way to starve Afghanistan's people and retard the nation's development, they could have found no better formula than the heinous misogyny they institutionalized. Women are the key to food security. By persecuting them, the Taliban made it impossible for women, especially widows, to care for themselves and their children. By now the details of the Taliban's domestic terrorism against women are well known: no medical care, no education, no income-generating work, no freedom of movement, no exit from the prison their own homes became. This policy feminized poverty and deepened a vicious cycle of pauperization produced by decades of war.

Gender inequality in rights and in access to resources imposes huge costs on the health and well-being of entire societies. In an influential 1990 article, Amartya Sen coined the term "missing women" to describe the great numbers of women in the world who are literally not alive due to family neglect and discrimination. Sen estimated that worldwide there are 100 million missing women, half of whom are in South Asia. Widespread neglect of girls' and women's health, nutrition, education, and care yields high female morbidity and mortality and high child malnutrition.

Women's Status and Child Nutrition

New work by Food Consumption and Nutrition Division (FCND) research fellow Lisa Smith, FCND director Lawrence Haddad, and Emory University collaborators has established the link between women's status and child nutrition. "We've actually been able to show that the low status of women in many Asian countries affects babies," Smith says. She is careful to distinguish between women's health, an important factor in child survival, and women's status, "which refers to women's power relative to men, in the households, communities, and nations in which they live. Power is the ability to make choices for oneself and one's family," she says. "When women's power relative to men is low, they have less control of their own time and household income; their time constraints are tighter and they lack social supports; their knowledge and beliefs are limited due to less exposure to education and information; their mental health, confidence, and self-esteem suffer; their autonomy and freedom of movement may be severely circumscribed; and their access to female-specific health services may be inadequate."

The researchers constructed an index of women's decision making power relative to their husbands', including household-level data on whether the woman works for cash, the age of the woman at marriage, and the age and educational differences between husband and wife. Whatever a woman's power relative to men's within the household, women may encounter various barriers outside the home: fewer work opportunities, lower wages, and a narrower range of acceptable behavior. For this reason, the researchers also included a community-level measure of women's status.

Women's nutrition, which Smith et al. found to be strongly associated with status, directly affects the health and nutrition of children. It is well known that poor prenatal maternal nutrition leads to low birth weight, which is the single most important predictor of child survival, and that micronutrient malnutrition affects the pre- and post-natal health of the child. "Women's nutrition affects their energy levels and their ability to breastfeed and carry out essential child care," Smith says. "Care for women, including prenatal and birthing care, is an important pathway through which women's status affects child nutrition."

Women's status also affects child nutrition through the quality of a mother's care for her children. "Although women

Three Reasons to Empower Women

Women's well-being is key to the overall health of a society. Women often eat last and least, even when pregnant or nursing. Undernourished women give birth to undernourished children, and this cycle continues.

Women's productivity: Women produce 80 percent of the food in Africa, more than 50 percent in South Asia, and more than 40 percent in Latin America, yet they are largely denied access to the training, credit, tools and other inputs they need.

Women's leadership: Given women's responsibilities, when they have a voice in the decisions that affect their lives, they are key change agents in setting the agenda for development.

"Empowering Women Is Critical to Ending Hunger,"
The Hunger Project, April 2002. www.thp.org.

with lower status tend to breastfeed more, the food they give their children is of lower quality; the timing and frequency of feedings is not what's needed for optimal child development; and the health-seeking practices on behalf of children are curtailed," Smith says. "If a woman can't leave the house, she can't immunize or get medical care for her children."

It isn't enough to care for children, important as that is. Women must be cared for too. Smith's research concludes that in regions where women's status is low, the impacts of programs to improve care practices for children, such as child feeding, would be more sustainable when combined with efforts to improve women's status.

Education of Women as a Factor

Women's education is an important determinant of a child's nutritional status. An earlier study of 63 developing countries by Smith and Haddad shows that gains in women's education accounted for 43 percent of the decline in child malnutrition between 1970 and 1995. Across the developing world, there is a strong positive correlation between mothers' average schooling and child survival.

A study by IFPRI researchers Agnes Quisumbing and John Maluccio in Bangladesh, Indonesia, Ethiopia, and South Africa shows that when women control assets, expenditures on children's education increase and the rate of illness among girls drops. Another Quisumbing study finds that increasing the education and input levels of female farmers to those of male farmers in Sub-Saharan Africa could increase yields as much as 22 percent. In Ivory Coast, John Hoddinott of Dalhousie University and Lawrence Haddad find that increasing women's share of cash income in the household significantly raises the share of the household budget allocated to food and reduces the share spent on alcohol and cigarettes.

"The empowerment of women tends to reduce child neglect and mortality, cut down fertility and overcrowding, and broaden social concerns ... " according to Amartya Sen. IFPRI studies support this view and constitute a strong argument that improving women's status and education is necessary to attain and maintain food security and other development objectives. The human rights of women cannot wait until other economic milestones or development goals have been met. Rather, study after study confirms what should be obvious: Guaranteeing women's human rights is crucial for development and a pathway to economic prosperity.

> *"Often the cause of [geriatric] malnu-trition isn't a single event but a cas-cade of problems that include physical, social and psychological issues."*

Aging Causes Malnutrition

Christine Facciolo

Christine Facciolo is a reporter and contributor to the Delaware News Journal. *In the following viewpoint, she maintains that malnutrition is a serious problem for the elderly population. She enumerates physical, social, and economic factors that cause malnutrition in the elderly, and offers suggestions for how care-givers can stay vigilant and alleviate malnutrition.*

As you read, consider the following questions:

1. According to the Nutrition Screening Initiative, what percentage of community-dwelling seniors is undernour-ished?
2. What physical factors can cause malnutrition in the elderly?
3. What social factors contribute to malnutrition in the elderly?

Christine Facciolo, "Diet Alone Not Enough for Geriatric Nutrition," *Delaware Online*, January 15, 2008. Reproduced by permission.

Ethel Clark knows more than a thing or two about the relationship between proper nutrition and good health. The active nonagenarian studied home economics at Cornell University and has been living what she learned since graduating in 1931.

The results are impressive. At 97, she has her own apartment at Forwood Manor in Brandywine Hundred, where she participates in a full slate of activities. She maintains an optimal weight and takes no medications. Her gait is so swift that residents and staff have nicknamed her "speed demon."

Clark is one of an elite group of seniors healthy enough to care for themselves. But a closer look at many of Clark's contemporaries would likely reveal a host of nutritional problems that can adversely affect their health and their ability to maintain independence.

"Good nutrition is important at every stage of life," said Kimberly Kauffman, a clinical dietitian with Christiana Care Health System.

Yet many seniors eat so poorly that they are at serious risk for malnutrition, according to Dr. Jeffrey Blumberg, director of the Antioxidants Research Laboratory at the Friedman School of Nutrition Science and Policy at Tufts University. Indeed, the Nutrition Screening Initiative, a multidisciplinary coalition headed by the American Dietetic Association and the American Academy of Family Physicians, estimates that 20 percent to 60 percent of the community-dwelling elderly are undernourished.

Obesity is also common among the elderly. But experts warn that plump doesn't necessarily mean well-nourished. "When you look at an obese person, what you're seeing by and large is fat," said Deanna Rolland, a registered dietitian and president-elect of the Delaware Dietetic Association. "You have no idea what's going on with muscle mass. They could be starving for protein."

Many Factors Can Have a Negative Effect

Malnutrition is a general term that can apply to both an inadequate or excessive intake of calories and nutrients. This potentially life-threatening condition is caused by gross deficiencies in calories and protein or by the stress of trauma, fever, and surgery. Symptoms include physical wasting, low body-mass index and low levels of albumin and other serum blood proteins.

But while physicians readily acknowledge the importance of good nutrition in managing and preventing chronic disease in the elderly, few provide nutritional assessments in office-based settings, according to the Nutrition Screening Initiative. What's more, the earliest signs of malnutrition—lethargy, fatigue and weakness—are often dismissed as part of the normal aging process.

"If a person tells their doctor that they're feeling tired, the doctor might say, 'You're 74, what do you expect,'" Blumberg said.

There's also debate over what constitutes the recommended daily requirements for the elderly. "We have people who are 80-plus that we don't have any numbers on," Rolland said. "When they did the [recommended daily allowances] initially, they were talking about the 'elderly' being 51 and over."

The amount of energy, or calories, the body needs decreases with age because of changes in metabolism. As the body ages, it loses bone and muscle and gains fat. Calorie needs decrease significantly because of more body fat and less lean muscle, as well as less physical activity.

But as the need for calories decreases, the need for protein, vitamins and minerals remains the same and might even increase because of illness, injury, stress, malabsorption and a weakened immune system, said Dr. Christine Gerbstadt, who also is a registered dietitian and spokeswoman for the American Dietetic Association.

"Unlike a younger person, the senior must make every calorie count by choosing nutrient-dense foods and reserve cakes and candies as occasional treats," she said.

Other Issues Involved

Often the cause of [geriatric] malnutrition isn't a single event but a cascade of problems that include physical, social and psychological issues.

Many older people suffer from debilitating chronic illnesses, making it difficult for them to shop, prepare meals or even feed themselves. Their medications can suppress the appetite even as they increase the body's nutritional needs, Gerbstadt said.

Dental problems, including gum disease, tooth loss and ill-fitting dentures, can make chewing nutrient-rich foods such as meat, fruit and vegetables difficult, said Christiana Care geriatrician Dr. Ina I. Li. Neurological disorders can interfere with swallowing.

Age-related changes in the gastrointestinal tract can affect the way the body absorbs and uses nutrients, Kauffman said. As people age, the production of certain digestive enzymes and acids slows down, interfering with protein breakdown and the absorption of vitamin B-12, folate, calcium, and iron. A vitamin B-12 deficiency can have devastating effects on the nervous system, causing mental confusion, unsteady gait, muscle weakness, slurred speech and psychosis, symptoms associated with disorders such as Parkinson's and Alzheimer's.

Aging also is associated with a general decline in gut motility that can cause constipation, Li said. A sedentary lifestyle and lack of fiber-rich foods aggravate the problem.

Elderly shut-ins are at an increased risk for vitamin D deficiency that can further impede calcium absorption, Kauffman said. Active seniors can be at risk because aging reduces the skin's ability to synthesize the vitamin.

Even among healthy people, the senses of taste and smell fade with age, robbing food of much of its flavor. As a result, seniors tend to favor foods that are very sweet or salty, which can lead to some poor nutritional choices, Li said. In addition, the ability to sense thirst also declines with age, putting many seniors at risk for dehydration.

Meanwhile, the threat of "drug-induced malnutrition" is underappreciated, Blumberg said. Many drugs alone or in combination harm nutrition by altering appetite or taste, causing nausea or hampering the body's ability to absorb nutrients.

Social and Economic Factors

Social and economic factors can also lead to malnutrition, experts note. Seniors living on limited fixed incomes often have to choose between nutritious foods and life-saving medications.

Even with adequate resources, getting groceries from the store to home can be a challenge. "It's hard enough to a younger person to lug groceries on and off a bus, let alone a senior," Rolland said.

Although no one knows for sure how many seniors suffer from alcohol-related problems, many experts agree the number is probably significant. Alcohol is a leading contributor to malnutrition, since it decreases appetite, destroys nutrients and often substitutes for meals, Blumberg said.

Isolation, and the loneliness and depression that often accompany it, can also contribute to malnutrition. People living alone often don't feel like cooking, so they grab anything that's convenient, Li said.

Ensure Healthy Habits

Malnutrition can be a serious problem, but seniors and their caregivers can take steps to promote healthy eating habits.

Factors Influencing Nutritional Inadequacy in the Elderly Population

Physiologic	Pathologic
Decreased taste	Dentition
Decreased smell	Dysphagis, swallowing problems
Dysregulation of satiation	Diseases (cancer, CHF, COPD, diabetes, ESRD, thyroid)
Delayed gastric emptying	Medications (diuretic, antihypertensive, dopamine, agonist, antidepressant, antibiotic, antihistamine)
Decreased gastric acid	Alcoholism
Decreased lean body mass	Dementia

Sociologic	Psychologic
Ability to shop for food	Depression
Ability to prepare food	Anxiety
Financial status low socioeconomic	Loneliness
Impaired activities of daily living skills	Emotionally stressful life events
Lack of interactions with others at mealtime	Grief
	Dysphoria

CHF = congestive heart failure
COPD = chronic obstructive pulmonary disease
ESRD = end-stage renal disease

TAKEN FROM: Carol Evans, "Malnutrition in the Elderly: A Multifactorial Failure to Thrive," *The Permanente Journal,* Spring 2005.

First, try making meals a social event. This may be the most important step toward preventing malnutrition. Older people clearly do better when they have company, experts note.

Planning healthy between-meal snacks can help, too. Bill Burich, 93, of Forwood Manor, said he's opting for smaller, more frequent feedings because he noticed his appetite isn't as large as it once was. "I'll have a glass of V8 or some cheese," he said. "At bedtime, I'll have a piece of raisin toast and a glass of milk."

Burich drinks several glasses of milk a day for protein and keeps nutritional supplements on hand. He also makes a point to exercise daily, alternating walking with resistance training to maintain lean muscle.

Evan and Ann Houseman are making an effort to incorporate more nutrient-rich foods into their diets. Both diabetics in their early 70s, they prepare most of their meals in their cottage at Cokesbury Village, choosing from fish, poultry and whole grains and cutting down on carbohydrates and sweets. Evan also runs a couple of miles a day on the treadmill while Ann works as a docent. They've managed to keep their weight down and have enough energy to chase their grandchildren, which makes them happy, Ann said.

Evelyn Smith has followed a healthy diet throughout most of her adult life and vowed to continue as she grew older.

"I always said I wanted to make sure I continued to eat well, because I didn't want to become one of those people who got older and got into the habit of not eating," said Smith, who is in her mid-70s and lives independently in her Belvedere home. "I know that happens to a lot of people."

Although Smith keeps to a diet rich in fruits and vegetables, she finds herself reading more labels these days, checking for sodium content, counting carbohydrates and making sure the bread she buys is 100 percent whole wheat. She also includes more protein in her diet by incorporating more cottage cheese, nuts, soy milk and natural peanut butter into her meals.

Keep Up-to-Date on Latest Developments

Clark has made it a point to keep up with the latest developments in nutrition research. "I've read all kinds of newsletters about what they're doing with nutrition at the various universities," she said.

While she's always made an effort to eat well, she said she can be more flexible in her food choices than a lot of seniors. "I've been blessed," she said. "I have good blood pressure and the rest of those things, and I don't take any medications."

Still, she makes sure her diet includes daily servings of whole grains, proteins and fruits and vegetables. One thing that has changed: She occasionally eats smaller, mere frequent meals because she's noticed her appetite has decreased.

"I rarely finish a full entrée, because I'm full, and there's no sense in forcing yourself," said Clark, who also keeps nutritional supplements on hand for late-night snacks.

Good nutrition helps give her the energy she needs to pursue her activities at Forwood Manor, where she chairs the crafts committee and teaches knitting.

"I've made over 600 caps for the preemies at the hospital," Clark said.

> "Nutritional status is compromised where people are exposed to high levels of infection due to unsafe and insufficient water supply and inadequate sanitation."

Dirty Water and Poor Sanitation Are Root Causes of Malnutrition

World Health Organization (WHO)

The World Health Organization (WHO) is the directing and co-ordinating arm of the United Nations on health matters, responsible for providing leadership on global health matters. In the following viewpoint, WHO stresses how important a safe, clean water supply and adequate sanitation are to maintaining nutritional levels.

As you read, consider the following questions:

1. How does this World Health Organization viewpoint define malnutrition?
2. According to the viewpoint, how does dirty water and poor sanitation increase the risk of malnutrition?

3. Malnutrition affects how many people out of every three worldwide, according to WHO statistics?

Malnutrition is a major health problem, especially in developing countries. Water supply, sanitation, and hygiene given their direct impact on infectious disease, especially diarrhoea, are important for preventing malnutrition. Both malnutrition and inadequate water supply and sanitation are linked to poverty. The impact of repeated or persistent diarrhoea on nutrition-related poverty and the effect of malnutrition on susceptibility to infectious diarrhoea are reinforcing elements of the same vicious circle, especially amongst children in developing countries.

The Disease and How It Affects People

Malnutrition essentially means "bad nourishment". It concerns not enough as well as too much food, the wrong types of food, and the body's response to a wide range of infections that result in malabsorption of nutrients or the inability to use nutrients properly to maintain health. Clinically, malnutrition is characterized by inadequate or excess intake of protein, energy, and micronutrients such as vitamins, and the frequent infections and disorders that result.

People are malnourished if they are unable to utilize fully the food they eat, for example due to diarrhoea or other illnesses (secondary malnutrition), if they consume too many calories (overnutrition), or if their diet does not provide adequate calories and protein for growth and maintenance (undernutrition or protein-energy malnutrition).

Malnutrition in all its forms increases the risk of disease and early death. Protein-energy malnutrition, for example, plays a major role in half of all under-five deaths each year in developing countries. Severe forms of malnutrition include marasmus (chronic wasting of fat, muscle and other tissues); cretinism and irreversible brain damage due to iodine defi-

Diarrhoea Is Linked to Dirty Water and Poor Sanitation

- 1.8 million people die every year from diarrhoeal diseases (including cholera); 90% are children under 5, mostly in developing countries.

- 88% of diarrhoeal disease is attributed to unsafe water supply, inadequate sanitation and hygiene.

- Improved water supply reduces diarrhoea morbidity by 21%.

- Improved sanitation reduces diarrhoea morbidity by 37.5%.

- The simple act of washing hands at critical times can reduce the number of diarrhoeal cases by up to 35%.

- Additional improvement of drinking-water quality, such as point of use disinfection, would lead to a reductio n of diarrhoea episodes of 45%.

World Health Organization, "Water, Sanitation, and Hygiene Links to Health: Facts and Figures," March 2004. www.who.int.

ciency; and blindness and increased risk of infection and death from vitamin A deficiency.

Nutritional status is compromised where people are exposed to high levels of infection due to unsafe and insufficient water supply and inadequate sanitation. In secondary malnutrition, people suffering from diarrhoea will not benefit fully from food because frequent stools prevent adequate absorption of nutrients. Moreover, those who are already experiencing protein-energy malnutrition are more susceptible to, and less able to recover from, infectious diseases.

The Cause

Individual nutritional status depends on the interaction between food that is eaten, the overall state of health and the physical environment. Malnutrition is both a medical and a social disorder, often rooted in poverty. Combined with poverty, malnutrition contributes to a downward spiral that is fuelled by an increased burden of disease, stunted development, and reduced ability to work. Poor water and sanitation are important determinants in this connection, but sometimes improvements do not benefit the entire population, for example where only the wealthy can afford better drinking-water supplies or where irrigation is used to produce export crops. Civil conflicts and wars, by damaging water infrastructure and contaminating supplies, contribute to increased malnutrition.

Scope of the Problem

Chronic food deficits affect about 792 million people in the world, including 20 percent of the population in developing countries. Worldwide, malnutrition affects one in three people and each of its major forms dwarfs most other diseases globally. Malnutrition affects all age groups, but it is especially common among the poor and those with inadequate access to health education and to clean water and good sanitation. More than 70 percent of children with protein-energy malnutrition live in Asia, 26 percent live in Africa, and 4 percent in Latin America and the Caribbean.

Interventions

Interventions that contribute to preventing malnutrition include:

- Improved water supply, sanitation, and hygiene.

- Health education for a healthy diet.

- Improved access, by the poor, to adequate amounts of healthy food.

- Ensuring that industrial and agricultural development do not result in increased malnutrition.

> *"That global warming policy is more likely a contributor than global warming itself is a strong enough reason to rethink this [biofuel] policy."*

Biofuels Contribute to the Problem of Malnutrition

Ben Lieberman

Ben Lieberman is senior policy analyst in the Thomas A. Roe Institute for Economic Policy Studies at the Heritage Foundation. In the following viewpoint, he maintains that global warming policies, in particular biofuel mandates, are in most cases more dangerous for the environment than the problem of global warming. He also maintains that biofuels are responsible for the widespread food crises and the resulting malnutrition that have been plaguing developing societies in recent years.

As you read, consider the following questions:

1. According to Lieberman, why is the connection between global warming and a tightening food supply exaggerated?

2. What are the problems with diverting agricultural products, like corn, to be used as biofuels, according to the author?

Ben Lieberman, "The Biofuel Dilemma," FrontPageMag.com, May 8, 2008. Reproduced by permission.

3. According to the U.S. mandate on biofuels, how many billion gallons of biofuels will America be using by 2022?

There are risks to global warming policy as well as risks to global warming, and although the former could be costlier than the latter, they are often neglected in climate change debate. While it may seem far-fetched to some that responding to the "climate crisis" could do more harm than good, it is in fact already happening. Consider the biofuels mandate, which is contributing to the very global warming problems it was designed to prevent.

Global Warming and Hunger

Among the litany of scary predictions associated with global warming is the adverse impact on future food supplies. For example, the 2007 U.N. [United Nations] Intergovernmental Panel on Climate Change report states that by 2020, "agricultural production, including access to food, in many African countries is projected to be severely compromised." A frequently cited global warming study conducted for the Pentagon went one step further, outlining potential hunger-related political unrest and national security concerns and stating that "aggressive wars are likely to be fought over food, water, and energy." Environmental activists warn of crop failures adding to the waves of "climate refugees" fleeing areas that can no longer sustain them.

As with all global warming related gloom-and-doom predictions, there are reasons for doubt. For example, the temperature increases during the 1980s and 1990s, on which current global warming concerns are largely based, were accompanied by increases in food production.

Thus, the predicted link between warming and reduced food supplies is not based on past experience. And, even assuming that the planet warms as much as these scenarios predict, it may result in the agricultural sector finding methods to adapt to changing conditions in order that yields are not significantly reduced. Further, the link between global warming and increased drought, the main cause of the hypothesized decline in food supplies, is challenged by several researchers.

Nevertheless, as global warming activists continue to predict alarming food shortages occurring at some point in the future, many look around and see a tightening food supply today. Only it was not caused by global warming: It was caused in part by global warming policy, specifically the move toward using food as fuel.

Biofuels Mandates and Hunger

America's first mandatory policy to reduce global warming emissions is its biofuels mandate. Along with the national security and other perceived benefits, these agriculturally based alternative fuels were purported to have lower global warming emissions than the petroleum-derived gasoline or diesel fuel they displace. At the beginning of the decade, Al Gore said that "by tripling U.S. use of bioenergy and bioproducts by 2010, we can keep millions of tons of greenhouse gases out of the air. . . ."

Thanks to the 2007 energy bill signed into law by President [George W.] Bush last December, it is occurring even faster than Gore imagined. The U.S. is now required to mix 9 billion gallons of such fuels into the gasoline supply in 2008, up from less than 3 billion gallons in 2000. The mandate is mostly met by corn-based ethanol. Europe has also set similar targets for biofuels, mostly bio-diesel made from palm oil, rapeseed, or soybeans.

Not surprisingly, diverting crops from food to fuel use has raised food prices. At a little over $2 per bushel when the mandate was first effective, the price of corn has recently surged well above $5, due in large part to nearly a quarter of

Biofuels in the United States

Biofuels are liquid, solid, or gaseous fuels derived from renewable biological sources. Biomass can be burned directly for thermal energy or converted to other high-value energy sources including ethanol, biodiesel, methanol, hydrogen, or methane. Currently, ethanol from corn grain and biodiesel are the only biofuels produced in the United States on an industrial scale.

U.S. Department of Energy, Office of Science, "Biofuels for Transportation," July 2005. http://genomicsgtl.energy.gov.

the crops now being needed for fuel use. A host of corn-related foods, such as corn-fed meat and dairy, have seen sharp price increases. Wheat and soybeans are also up, partly as a result of fewer acres now being planted in favor of corn. European biodiesel mandates have had a similar impact.

A Purdue University study places the annual food cost increases for 2007 at $22 billion and estimates that "$15 billion of this increase is related to the recent surge in demand to use crops as fuel." That $15 billion calculates to an additional $130 per household in 2007, and food prices are considerably higher thus far in 2008.

Biofuels Spur Pressure on Food Prices

Other factors—high energy costs, below-average yields in some regions, growing world population, a weak dollar—have also impinged on food supplies and prices. However, most experts see the biofuels mandates as a substantial contributor, and one that exacerbates any other pressures on food costs.

With 800 million people at risk for hunger and malnutrition, the consequences are far more severe in developing nations than they are in developed nations. "When millions of people are going hungry, it's a crime against humanity that food should be diverted to biofuels," said Palaniappan Chidambaram, India's finance minister. World Bank President Robert Zoellick has acknowledged that "biofuels are no doubt a significant contributor" to high food costs, adding that "it is clearly the case that programs in Europe and the United States that have increased biofuel production have contributed to the added demand for food."

Even some of the political unrest described in the Pentagon study is starting to emerge. Rising prices have led to food-related rioting in several developing nations. While it is not possible to demonstrate conclusively that, this rioting would not have occurred if not for the biofuels mandates, it is far from speculative to assume that the increased pressures of the mandates on food prices were contributors. In any event, the rioters are clearly not responding to global warming, as there has been no additional warming in 2007 and thus far in 2008.

Moreover, all of this is occurring from biofuels usage that is only a fraction of what will be required in the years ahead. America is only one-quarter of the way toward the 36 billion gallon requirement by 2022 included in last December's [2007] big energy bill. The European Union also has plans to increase its biodiesel use, though it is now reconsidering this policy.

To add insult to injury, the global warming benefits of biofuels have been called into question. Two recent studies published in the journal *Science* conclude that, rather than reducing carbon dioxide and other greenhouse gas emissions, biofuels actually increase them. One study finds that clearing lands for energy crops creates a so-called carbon debt by "releasing 17 to 420 times more carbon dioxide than the annual greenhouse gas (GHG) reductions that these biofuels would provide by displacing fossil fuels," while the other projects "GHG emissions from corn ethanol nearly double those from gasoline for each km driven."

Last year [2007], a study conducted for the Organization for Economic Cooperation and Development, presciently entitled "Biofuels: Is The Cure Worse Than the Disease?" stated that "the rush to energy crops threatens to cause food shortages and damage to biodiversity with limited benefits." The authors were right. Oxfam, an international aid organization that has been very vocal about the threat of global warming, now concedes that "large-scale growth in biofuels demand has pushed up food prices and so far there is little evidence that it is reducing overall carbon emissions."

Global Warming Policy Causing Problems

The very food-related problems that we see today are much like the hypothesized future ones that were supposed to be caused by global warming. That global warming policy is more likely a contributor than global warming itself is a strong enough reason to rethink this policy.

For this reason, Congress should repeal its current biofuels mandate. In addition, as the Senate soon takes up debate on S. 2191, the major global warming bill, it should heed the biofuels lesson and avoid any measures that may also prove to be more trouble than they are worth.

> "In recent months, a flood of press reports, articles in scientific journals, and statements from international bureaucrats have suggested that ethanol is starving the world's poor, is a waste of government money, and is bad for the environment. These claims are simply not true; some are based on partial information, some on gross disinformation, but none of them can withstand close scrutiny."

Biofuels Are Not Causing Malnutrition

Robert E. Zubrin

Robert Zubrin is an aerospace engineer, senior fellow at the Foundation for Defense of Democracies, and a contributing editor to the New Atlantis. *He is also the author of* Energy Victory: Winning the War on Terror by Breaking Free of Oil. *In the following viewpoint, he claims that the recent charges that biofuels are driving up food prices and causing food emergencies all over the world are false and based on disinformation. In fact, he argues, corn grown for ethanol does not adversely affect the grow-*

Robert E. Zubrin, "In Defense of Biofuels," *The New Atlantis*, Spring 2008. Reproduced by permission.

ing of other crops. Zubrin concludes by asserting that other factors are causing rising food prices, not the growing biofuel industry.

As you read, consider the following questions:

1. According to the author, what is the most prominent and immediately promising type of biofuel?
2. How many billion gallons of ethanol did the United States produce in 2007?
3. What are the two primary reasons for rising food prices, according to Zubrin?

On the world markets, the cost of a barrel of oil is, at this writing [2008], over $120. In the United States, a gallon of gasoline now costs, on average, roughly $3.50. Even when adjusted for inflation, both of those figures are now higher than they have ever been—higher than during the 1973 oil embargo, higher than during any subsequent peak. And yet, bizarrely, instead of focusing their attention on the staggering cost of oil and its ruinous implications for global growth and economic well-being, American policy makers and energy analysts have begun to decry a different fuel—one that holds the key to ending our dependency on expensive oil purchased from countries with interests inimical to our own.

Biofuels—a class of fuels of which ethanol is the most prominent and immediately promising—can play a central part in weaning the United States from oil. But in recent months, a flood of press reports, articles in scientific journals, and statements from international bureaucrats have suggested that ethanol is starving the world's poor, is a waste of government money, and is bad for the environment. These claims are simply not true; some are based on partial information, some on gross disinformation, but none of them can withstand close scrutiny. Many of the critics of ethanol mean well: They are worried about hungry children or big government.

Others have more self-interested motivations for their criticism of biofuels—like Hugo Chávez, the preening, obstreperous dictator of oil-exporting Venezuela, who has called ethanol production a "crime." Still others are driven by a Malthusian vision of a world with fewer people in it. No matter the motivations of these unlikeliest of bedfellows, their recent objections to ethanol could have the cumulative effect of warping U.S. and international biofuels policy—and just at the moment when exorbitant oil costs should, if anything, be leading legislators to adopt the critical technology needed to expand the role of biofuels in the world's fuel supply. . . .

Fueling Fears About Food

Hoping to reduce at least in some small way their need for oil, several countries have adopted energy policies requiring that a percentage of their national fuel supplies consist of biofuels. The European Union, for instance, is aiming to have biofuels make up 10 percent of its vehicle fuel supply by the year 2020. In the United States, legislation in 2005 and 2007 set mandates for ethanol in the nation's fuel mix; the current plan is to ramp up biofuels production until 36 billion gallons are mixed into the nation's fuel supply by 2022.

Unsurprisingly, the result of these mandates has been the rapid expansion of the nation's ethanol industry. The United States, which produced 3 billion gallons of ethanol in 2002, grew its production to 8 billion gallons in 2007, replacing some 5 percent of our gasoline supply. But while this seems like it would be cause for celebration—with enterprising and innovative American farmers helping to reduce our oil usage—some critics have recently alleged that the world's biofuels programs, especially the U.S. corn ethanol effort, are starving poor people around the world by reducing supply and driving up food prices. International bureaucrats have been the most vocal critics. A recent World Bank report claimed that "increased biofuel production has contributed to the rise in food prices." The U.N.'s Special Rapporteur on the Right to Food denounced biofuel production as "a crime against humanity." Jeffrey Sachs, a Columbia University economist who is an advisor to U.N. Secretary-General Ban Ki-moon, has said "we need to cut back significantly on our biofuels programs" because they are "a huge blow to the world food supply." It seems so obvious: With so much corn being turned into fuel, food shortages must inevitably result, and biofuels programs must be the cause.

The problem is, that's completely untrue.

Facts About Biofuels

Here are the facts. In the last five years, despite the nearly threefold growth of the corn ethanol industry—actually, because of it—the amount of corn grown in the United States has vastly increased. The U.S. corn crop grew by 45 percent, the production of distillers grain (a high-value animal feed made from the protein saved from the corn used for ethanol) quadrupled, and the net U.S. corn production of food for humans and feed for animals increased 34 percent.

Contrary to claims that farmers have cut other crops to grow more corn, U.S. soybean plantings this year [in 2008] are expected to be up 18 percent and wheat plantings up 6 percent. U.S. farm exports are up 23 percent over last year. America is clearly doing its share in feeding the world.

At bottom, the entire food versus fuel argument boils down to a Malthusian conceit—that there is only so much that can be grown, so if we grow more of one thing, we must necessarily grow less of something else. But this is simply false. Agriculture is not a zero-sum game. [There] are roughly 2,250 million acres of land in the continental United States. About 1,600 million of those acres are arable. Roughly half of that land (800 million acres) is farmland, but only about a third of that (280 million acres) is actually being cultivated. Only about 85 million of those farm acres are presently grow-

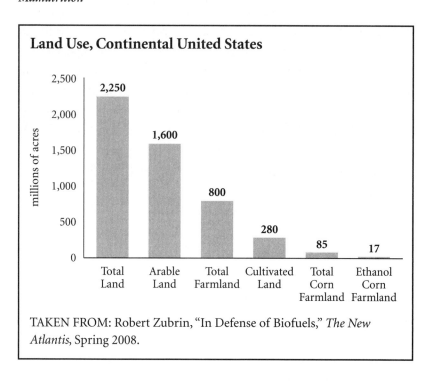

Land Use, Continental United States

TAKEN FROM: Robert Zubrin, "In Defense of Biofuels," *The New Atlantis*, Spring 2008.

ing corn, and just a fifth of that land—about 17 million acres—is growing corn that becomes ethanol. In short, there is plenty of farmland in the United States that could be used to grow more corn—or more of the other staple crops needed to meet domestic or international demand. Even more importantly, agricultural technology is constantly advancing. U.S. corn yields per acre have risen 17 percent since 2002, and the state of Iowa alone today produces more corn than the entire nation did in the 1940s. Applied globally, such improved techniques can multiply world agricultural yields many times. In fact, they have risen by a factor of six since 1930—which is why, even though the world's population has tripled since that time, there is a lot more food for everyone today.

So while it is true that there is now much more corn being used for ethanol than ever before, there is also much more total corn than ever before, including much more for food and feed than ever before, and still plenty of land, and room for implementation of improved methods to grow yet more.

But if biofuels aren't to blame for the rising food prices, what is?

What Is Causing High Food Prices?

In fact, there are several culprits. One is low farm productivity in some parts of the world. Regional droughts is another. Sometimes there is a confluence of factors: Some critics have foolishly claimed that recent food riots in Haiti could be linked to the U.S. ethanol mandate even though those riots were about rice, which the U.S. doesn't use to make ethanol, and were largely caused by unwise trade policies and a drought in Australia that, according to the *St. Petersburg Times*, "has seen [its] rice production fall by a stunning 98 percent."

But the two primary reasons for higher food prices are, first, higher demand, and second, higher fuel prices. The increased global demand for food ought to be seen as a very good thing: It represents hundreds of millions of people, especially in China and India, rising out of poverty and moving to more calorie-rich diets. Escalating fuel prices, however, are not good news: They drive up the cost of everything we eat. For example, consider the $3 box of cornflakes you might see in your grocery store. Farm commodity prices basically have a trivial effect on its price. A bushel of corn contains 56 pounds of grain, so at the current "very high" commodity price of $5 per bushel, a pound of corn costs 9 cents. So the 16 ounces of corn in that cereal box cost a total of 9 cents when bought from the farmer. But when the price of oil goes up, that increases the cost of production, transport, wages, and packaging—all driving up the retail cost of food.

And, in this regard, biofuels have already done more good than harm to the world's poor. According to the *Wall Street Journal*, "Global production of biofuels is rising annually by the equivalent of about 300,000 barrels of oil a day. That goes a long way toward meeting the growing demand for oil, which last year rose by about 900,000 barrels a day." The paper cites a Merrill Lynch analyst who "says that oil and gasoline prices would be about 15 percent higher if biofuel producers weren't increasing their output." So even though the world's biofuels industry is still just aborning, it has already begun to bring down oil prices.

> "Most of the effects of climate change are likely to be harmful ones: declining agricultural production and more hungry people, increased spread of infectious diseases, dangerous heat waves and floods."

Global Warming Is Causing Malnutrition

Sarah DeWeerdt

The World Watch Institute is an independent research organization that provides sustainability analyses for governments, businesses, and academia. In the following viewpoint, environmental writer Sarah DeWeerdt claims that global warming will increase malnutrition in poor tropical nations that are most vulnerable and the least responsible for causing it.

As you read, consider the following questions:

1. According to World Health Organization studies, how many people will global warming kill a year by 2020?
2. What regions of the world are most likely to be negatively affected by climate change?

3. Why will malnutrition increase as global warming worsens, according to the author?

Since the 1970s, rainfall has been scarce in the Sahel, the wide belt of semi-arid land that stretches across Africa on the southern edge of the Sahara Desert. One of the worst-affected areas has been the Tigray region of northern Ethiopia, where a series of prolonged droughts exacerbated by war caused widespread famine in the 1970s and 1980s.

To help increase the productivity of farmers' fields, the local government decided in the late 1980s to build a series of small dams to trap the unreliable rainfall and connect these to simple irrigation systems. Sure enough, harvests increased and fewer people went hungry—but health researchers also found that children in villages near the dams were seven times as likely to suffer from malaria. The water stored behind the dams provided perfect breeding habitat for the mosquitoes that carry the disease.

Global Warming's Effects on Populations

The people of this isolated rural region of Ethiopia offer a glimpse into the human future—a view of how global climate change can play havoc with populations' lives and livelihoods, and how addressing one climate-related problem can sometimes cause another. The World Health Organization (WHO) has calculated that by 2020 human-triggered climate change could kill 300,000 people worldwide every year. By 2000, in fact, climate change was already responsible for 150,000 excess deaths annually—deaths that wouldn't have occurred if we humans weren't burning vast quantities of fossil fuels and loading up the air with carbon dioxide and other greenhouse gases.

Jonathan Patz, a professor with the University of Wisconsin/Madison's Center for Sustainability and the Global Environment, praises the WHO's sober accounting as the most comprehensive, scientific estimate available of the health effects of climate change. The agency combined models of recent and projected climate change with data on several health dangers that are known to be affected by climate (including malaria, diarrheal diseases, and malnutrition) to calculate the disease burden due to changes in climate. However, Patz says, "their estimate is extremely conservative." Not only are the underlying assumptions conservative, but the analysis only concerns a few of the relatively better-understood health risks of climate change.

Climate change might have a few pluses for our species—for example, warmer winters probably mean fewer cold-related deaths in North America and Europe, while in some parts of the tropics hotter and drier conditions could reduce the survival of disease-carrying mosquitoes. But most of the effects of climate change are likely to be harmful ones: declining agricultural production and more hungry people, increased spread of infectious diseases, dangerous heat waves and floods. Although no region of the globe will be entirely spared, the negative effects are likely to fall most heavily on poor nations in tropical and subtropical regions. In other words, the people most vulnerable to the effects of climate change are precisely those who are least responsible for causing it—and those who have the least resources with which to adapt to it.

Changes in Food Production

"Malnutrition will very likely be one of the biggest impacts in low-income countries," says Kristie Ebi, an environmental consultant who has served on the Intergovernmental Panel on Climate Change (IPCC) and several other climate-change-related scientific bodies. Globally, food production is likely to decrease only modestly at worst, but this overall pattern hides what many researchers see as a growing inequality between the haves and have-nots of the world.

Effects of Climate Change on Health

- Increasing frequencies of heat waves: Recent analyses show that human-induced climate change significantly increased the likelihood of the European summer heat wave of 2003.

- More variable precipitation patterns are likely to compromise the supply of fresh water, increasing risks of water-borne disease.

- Rising temperatures and variable precipitation are likely to decrease the production of staple foods in many of the poorest regions, increasing risks of malnutrition.

- Rising sea levels increase the risk of coastal flooding, and may necessitate population displacement. More than half of the world's population now lives within 60 kilometers of the sea. Some of the most vulnerable regions are the Nile delta in Egypt, the Ganges-Brahmaputra delta in Bangladesh, and many small islands, such as the Maldives, the Marshall Islands and Tuvalu.

World Health Organization,
"Climate and Health," Fact Sheet 266,
August 2007. www.who.int.

Some relatively wealthy countries in temperate regions will likely see crop yields rise, mainly due to longer, warmer growing seasons. Even the excess carbon dioxide in the air that is the underlying cause of climate change can theoretically be a boon for agriculture, acting as a fertilizer when other conditions for plant growth are favorable. Though it's not yet clear whether or how this effect of carbon dioxide will play out in the real world, any beneficial effects are most likely to be seen at middle and high latitudes. The prospect of these changes causes skeptics of climate-change doom and gloom to envision vast stretches of northern tundra transformed into a future breadbasket.

Meanwhile, however, crop yields are likely to fall in the tropical and subtropical world, latitudes with many poorer countries where most of the world's hungry and malnourished live today. There, many crops are already growing near the upper bound of their temperature tolerance, so further warming would push them beyond their limits. In some areas, precipitation may increase, causing crops to rot; elsewhere, rainfall may diminish and become more erratic, arriving unpredictably as intense downpours that will run off the parched earth instead of nourishing the soil. And since the economies of many poorer countries are heavily dependent on agriculture, the failure of crops at home will leave them unable to buy surplus grain abroad.

For the last decade and a half, Martin Parry of the U.K. Met (formerly Meteorological) Office (and current co-chair of the IPCC working group on impacts of climate change), Cynthia Rosenzweig of the Goddard Institute for Space Studies, and a large group of other researchers from various institutions have been modeling the possible effects of climate change on production of the world's staple grain crops: wheat, rice, maize, and soybeans. Their work integrates several complex computer models—of global climate, crop yields, world food trade, and various patterns of economic development and population growth—to predict future global agricultural production and the risk of hunger. One set of their calculations indicates that, accounting for future population growth, continued "business as usual" greenhouse gas emissions would increase the ranks of the hungry by 80 million by 2080, mostly in Africa and southern Asia.

Already there are hints that such projections are beginning to come true. Recently, Ebi worked on a U.S. Agency for International Development study of possible adaptations to climate change in Zignasso, a town of about 3,000 people in the main agricultural area of southern Mali. "It's gotten hotter. It's gotten drier," she says of the area's climate. "Farmers are seeing the rains come at somewhat different times of year," and sometimes there are dry spells during the rainy season. To combat declining soil quality farmers have started adding more fertilizer to their fields of potatoes, the main cash crop, but nevertheless climate shifts mean that harvests are getting smaller.

If average temperatures in this area of Mali increase, as expected, another 2–3°C by the 2060s, potato yields could further decrease by about a quarter. It's not clear whether rainfall in the area will increase or decrease. In general, scientists simply don't understand this part of the climate system very well, so different models often disagree in their predictions. But in either case, says Ebi, the soil will probably be drier, because warm temperatures cause soil moisture to evaporate more quickly—and that could spell trouble for rice, the area's staple grain crop.

As drier conditions shrink growing seasons in tropical and subtropical environments, farmers have been encouraged by governments and aid agencies to turn to new, fast-growing crop varieties: rice that matures in 90 days, for example, rather than 120 days. But this solution may beget its own set of problems, Ebi says: "The fast-growing cultivars, because they grow faster, have less time to absorb micronutrients" from the soil, so they might provide people with sufficient calories but leave them vulnerable to vitamin and mineral deficiencies. "We need to pay attention to the quality of the food, not just the quantity."

> *"There is no scientific basis for the notion that 'global warming' will increase malnutrition or famine by reducing the world's food supply."*

Global Warming Is Not Causing Malnutrition

Science & Public Policy Institute

The Science & Public Policy Institute is a nonprofit research institute that disseminates information about the energy and the environment, and urges a reappraisal of climate change policy. In the following viewpoint, the institute outlines four claims made about the effects of global warming in a 2008 World Health Organization report—including one about malnutrition—and presents evidence to debunk them.

As you read, consider the following questions:

1. What are the four global warming scares the Science & Public Policy Institute attempts to debunk in this viewpoint?

2. According to the viewpoint, why won't the World Health Organization (WHO) tell the truth that it is bad gov-

Science & Public Policy Institute, "'Global Warming' Is Causing Malaria, Floods, and Malnutrition," April 9, 2008. Reproduced by permission.

ernment—not global warming—that causes malnutrition in developing countries?

3. According to the authors, how has global warming impacted 300,000 kilometers of desert in the Southern Sudan in the past 30 years?

The scares: The World Health Organization [WHO] announced on 7 April 2008 that millions of Asians could face poverty, disease and hunger as a result of rising temperatures and increased rainfall. The WHO's regional director for Asia [Dr. Shigeru Omi] said that malaria, diarrhea, malnutrition, and floods cause an estimated 150,000 deaths annually in the region. A WHO adviser on malaria and other parasitic diseases added climate change in combination with unchecked human development has contributed to the problem.

Let's Examine the Scares

Scare 1: Mosquito-borne diseases. The WHO's spokesman said malaria-carrying mosquitoes represent the clearest telltale sign that global warming has begun to impact human health: They are now found in cooler climates such as South Korea and the highlands of Papua New Guinea. Warmer weather means that mosquitoes' breeding cycles are shortening, allowing them to multiply at a much faster rate, posing an even greater threat of disease, he told reporters in Manila.

The exceptionally high number in Asia of dengue cases, which are also spread by mosquitoes, could be due to rising temperatures and rainfall, but [Dr. Shigeru] Omi said more study is needed to establish connection between climate change and dengue. "Without urgent action through changes in human lifestyle, the effects of this phenomenon on the global climate system could be abrupt or even irreversible, sparing no country and causing more frequent and more intense heat waves, rain storms, tropical cyclones, and surges in sea level," he said.

Scare 2: Rising sea levels. In the Marshall Islands and South Pacific island nations, rising sea levels have already penetrated low-lying areas, submerging arable lands and causing migrations to New Zealand or Australia, he said.

Scare 3: Malnutrition. The WHO spokesman said poorer countries with meager resources and weak health systems will be hit hardest because malnutrition is already widespread, with the young, women and the elderly at particular risk.

Scare 4: Climate variability. He said unusual, unexpected climate patterns—too much rain or too little—have an impact on food production, especially irrigation crops such as rice, and can cause unemployment, economic upheavals and political unrest.

Here's the Truth

The truth: The WHO's announcement appears to have been timed deliberately to coincide with the launch of Al Gore's "$300 million" advertising campaign to whip up fear of "global warming". It lacks any scientific basis whatsoever, and seems to be yet another of the numerous rent-seeking exercises in which public authorities worldwide are indulging on the basis of the half-understood and flagrantly exaggerated climate scare.

Truth About Malaria

The truth about malaria. Malaria is not, repeat not, a tropical disease. The largest outbreak in the past 100 years was in the 1920s and 1930s in Siberia—not noted for its tropical climate. Some 13 million people were infected, of whom 600,000 died, 30,000 of them in Arkhangelsk, Russia's port on the Arctic Circle. The malaria mosquito, according to Professor Paul Reiter, the world's foremost expert, is capable of surviving in temperatures as low as −25 degrees Celsius (−13 degrees Fahrenheit). Its only dependence upon temperature is that, during the breeding season, it requires an ambient temperature of at least 15 degrees Celsius (59 degrees Fahrenheit). Since there has been no increase in mean global surface temperatures for the past ten years, the area of the planet where the temperature reaches 15 degrees Celsius during the breeding season has not increased: So there is no possible scientific basis for saying that the current high malaria mortality owes anything to "global warming".

The true reason why some 850,000 people a year—most of them children—die of malaria is the WHO's worldwide ban on the use of the one effective agent against the anopheles mosquito: DDT. The acronym "DDT" does not appear in the IPCC's [Intergovernmental Panel on Climate Change] ramblings about malaria: Yet the ban on [it] is the real reason why malaria has spread. Before DDT was banned a third of a century ago, it had proven so effective at killing malaria mosquitoes that the worldwide annual number of malaria deaths had fallen to just 50,000. After the ban was introduced at the instigation of the Democrat administration of John F. Kennedy in the US under pressure from the same environmentalists who are now peddling the "global warming" scare, malaria deaths rapidly rose to more than 1 million per year. It was only on 15 September 2006 that Dr. Arata Kochi of the WHO lifted the ban. He said:

> Quite often in this field politics comes first and science second. We must take a position based on the science and the data.

However, many countries refuse to use DDT even for interior spraying, where it cannot cause harm to any creature except the mosquito. It is entirely harmless to humans, who can eat it daily by the tablespoonful without any ill effects. The disastrous DDT ban killed approximately 40 million children before the WHO finally got around to ending the ban and recommending DDT. It is an excellent example of the reason why it is necessary to get the science right rather than acting

"The icecaps are melting!"

"The icecaps are melting!" Cartoon by Joseph Farris. www.CartoonStock.com.

upon the incompetent and exaggerated distortions of science that are routinely peddled by the lavishly funded but politically motivated environmental movement.

Likewise, there is no basis whatsoever in science for supposing that warmer weather will cause dengue fever to spread. End of scare 1.

Truth About Sea Levels

The truth about rising sea levels. The IPCC's 2007 report, confronted with evidence that sea level is not rising very fast, had to cut its high-end estimate of sea-level rise to 2100 by one-third, from 3 feet to under 2 feet. Its best estimate is that sea level will rise by just 1 [foot] 5 [inches] in 100 years, compared with 8 inches in the 20th century and a mean rate of 4 feet per century throughout the 10,000 years since the end of the last ice age.

Professor Niklas Moerner, the world's foremost expert on sea level, says that even the IPCC's central estimate is a baseless exaggeration. He sees no reason to expect a sea-level rise to 2100 of more than the 20 cm (8 inches) observed in the 20th century. The 20th-century rate of sea-level rise was one-sixth of the mean centennial rate. More than 90 percent of the world's ice is in Antarctica, and most of the Antarctic has cooled throughout the past 50 years, with a progressive accumulation of ice in most pads of the continent. Some 5 percent of the world's ice is in the vast Greenland ice sheet, whose mean thickness grew by 2 inches per year between 1993 and 2003. The remainder of the world's ice is in mountain glaciers, which began receding in 1880, long before the human effect on climate could have been significant, and have receded at a near-linear rate since. In the cold winter of 2007, many glaciers worldwide began advancing.

The main reason for imagining that warmer weather might cause sea level to rise has nothing to do with ice, therefore. It is thermosteric expansion of sea water that is the largest contributor to sea-level rise today. Yet this expansion can only occur if the oceans are warming, which they are not. So there is no scientific basis for the WHO's assertion that anthropogenic "global warming" is causing sea level to rise. In the Pacific atolls, which are the poster-children for this particular scare, the corals are capable of growing towards the light at ten times the rate of sea-level rise that is projected by the IPCC, so there is no reason to suppose that they will be inundated. It is, after all, not an accident that, after 400 feet of sea- level rise since the last ice age, all the atolls are exactly at or just above sea level. End of scare 2.

Truth About Malnutrition

The truth about malnutrition. There has never been a famine in a country that is fully and functionally democratic in the Western sense. Famine and malnutrition are caused by one thing and one thing alone: bad government. The WHO is a division of the UN, and the UN is in effect a dictators' club, so the WHO cannot say that it is bad government that is causing malnutrition. So in common with public authorities worldwide, it lays the blame for what are, at root, failures of governmental administration upon "global warming".

There is no scientific basis for the notion that "global warming" will increase malnutrition or famine by reducing the world's food supply. As the world warms, the climate becomes generally wetter, providing irrigation of crops in areas that have not been farmed for centuries. In the southern Sahara, for instance, some 300,000 square kilometres of desert have given place to vegetation in the past 30 years. If the weather warms significantly, vast areas of currently barren tundra in Siberia, Alaska, and northern Canada will become available for cultivation, vastly increasing the world's usable agricultural land. Warmer weather has always improved the growth of crops, and will always do so. End of scare 3.

Truth About Climate Variability

The truth about climate variability. The climate varies naturally, has always done so, and will always do so. Even the excitable IPCC says that no individual extreme-weather event such as those so luridly described by the WHO can be ascribed to "global warming". The principal reason for the increase in the scale of climate-related disasters is not the increase in extreme-weather events: for there has been no such increase. The WHO mentions typhoons and tropical cyclones, but there has been no increase in hurricane frequency or intensity for 100 years, and the frequency of severe typhoons and tropical cyclones has decreased throughout the past 30 years. There is no basis either in theory or in observation for the notion that the climate has become any more unpredictable than it has always been. End of scare 4.

Periodical Bibliography

The following articles have been selected to supplement the diverse views presented in this chapter.

Ronald Bailey   "Feed SUVs and Starve People," *Reason Magazine*, June 22, 2007.

Ronald Bailey   "The Biggest Green Mistake," *Reason Magazine*, April 8, 2008.

Martha Burk   "Why a Food Crisis?" *Ms.*, Summer 2008.

Jon Entine   "Why Small Is Not Always Sustainable," June 16, 2008.www.aei.com.

Christopher Flavelle   "Good Crop, Bad Crop," *Slate*, July 10, 2008.

Newt Gingrich   "Ethanol: Pro and Con," *Atlanta Journal-Constitution*, April 18, 2008.

Kevin H. Hassett   "Food Crisis Shows How Bad Policies Can Be Deadly," April 21, 2008. www.bloomberg.com.

Ernest Istook   "Ethanol: The Political Fuel," April 18, 2008. www.heritage.org.

Scott Kilman   "Rising Food Costs Further Pressure Food Prices," *Wall Street Journal*, July 9, 2008.

Andrew Leonard   "The Battle over Biofuels," *Salon*, November 3, 2006.

Ben Lieberman   "Ethanol and Other Biofuels: A Global Warming Solution Worse than the Problem," May 2, 2008. www.heritage.org.

William Saletan   "Food Fight," *Slate*, July 7, 2007.

Daniel J. Weiss   "The Human Side of Global Warming," April
and Robin Pam   10, 2008. www.americanprogress.org.

OPPOSING
VIEWPOINTS®
SERIES

CHAPTER 3

Who Should Help Alleviate Malnutrition?

Chapter Preface

As the scourge of hunger and malnutrition continues into the twenty-first century, commentators debate who is responsible for ultimately addressing—and hopefully alleviating—the problem. Is it national, regional, or local governments, or international governmental organizations (known as IGOs)? Are private corporations better prepared to mobilize resources to fight malnutrition, or non-governmental organizations (NGOs)? Or do global partnerships between these bodies and organizations provide the best opportunity to save lives and eliminate malnutrition?

It would seem that national, regional, and local governments would be the obvious choices to confront the issue of malnutrition amongst its own population. Government is supposed to protect and provide for its citizens, and that would mean fighting hunger and malnutrition. As commentators point out, however, government programs are often inefficient and riddled with corruption. Some governments use hunger as a weapon to keep their citizens in line and too weak to fight, or take revenge on political enemies by destroying crops and bringing on famine and malnutrition.

IGOs are organizations like the World Health Organization (WHO), UNICEF (United Nations Children's Fund), and the Food and Agriculture Organization of the United Nations (FAO) that are governed by boards of member states and provide developmental assistance in areas severely affected by hunger and malnutrition. These organizations help countries use their own resources more effectively to eliminate food shortages and feed the hungry. Some commentators note, however, that IGOs are often hampered by political limitations in these member countries and have not devoted the money necessary to launch a full-scale plan to eliminate the problems of hunger and malnutrition.

NGOs are nonprofit groups or associations staffed by volunteers and independent of governmental institutions working to address serious problems, like malnutrition. NGOs such as Oxfam and ActionAid provide nutrition intervention and food aid, protect vulnerable populations from discriminatory trade practices and land schemes, and pressure governments to respond to malnutrition and hunger within their own borders. Commentators argue, however, that NGOs are often limited by political circumstances and their own resources.

In recent years, private industry has become involved in the fight against malnutrition on a number of levels, realizing that it is within their own best interests to help create healthy and productive workforces and marketplaces, and to garner goodwill in areas in which they are actively working to help the populace. Critics argue that the only responsibility a corporation truly has is to make a profit for its shareholders and that the recent Corporate Social Responsibility (CSR) Movement is a sham to generate good public relations in growing markets such as India and Africa.

Global partnerships are another option to fight malnutrition on a large scale. When business teams up with governments, NGOs, or IGOs, the potential to address wide-ranging and serious problems is staggering. In order to be successful, all parties must work in close collaboration and have the best interests of the people in mind—and critics argue that is not always the case, thereby creating an unproductive and potentially harmful situation.

To eradicate the global problem of malnutrition, all useful avenues must be explored and all available resources should be utilized. The viewpoints in this chapter examine which organizations or institutions are best equipped to effectively fight the malnutrition problem and provide answers in the twenty-first century.

> "While few would recommend a complete return to the interventionist policies of the past, many acknowledge the important role of the state in providing infrastructure and public goods to facilitate markets."

Government Has an Important Role in the Eradication of Malnutrition

Oxfam International

Oxfam International is an organization that works with partners and communities around the world to help developing nations, eradicating poverty, hunger, and malnutrition. In the following viewpoint, Oxfam asserts that the food crises and flawed market reforms in Africa in the 1980s proved the necessity of government intervention to ensure food security. It lists several ways governments can intervene to this end, but stresses that governments must strive to reduce the risks of corruption and political abuse.

Oxfam International, *Causing Hunger: An Overview of the Food Crisis in Africa.* Washington, DC: Oxfam International, 2006. © Oxfam International July 2006. Reproduced by permission.

As you read, consider the following questions:

1. How did free-market policies introduced in the 1980s in Africa fail to alleviate hunger and malnutrition?

2. According to Oxfam International, how can government interventions help fight hunger and malnutrition in Africa?

3. How did the Malawian government intervene to help its people grow more maize?

A significant lesson learned from the flawed market reforms introduced from the 1980s by the International Monetary Fund and World Bank, backed by major donors, is that state action is needed to deliver food security. This is particularly so in rural areas of Africa, where markets are often very weak, risky, and inequitable, and where price instability is a particular problem.

Free-market policies were supposed to eradicate the urban bias, inefficiency, and corruption associated with previous interventionist state policies. However, it is increasingly accepted that such policies have failed to deliver the substantial agricultural growth needed to drive rural poverty reduction and increase food security. After a pronounced decline in the 1970s and early 1980s, per capita food production has stagnated.

A major problem was the reduction of the state's capacity to intervene in food markets, without first assuring the emergence of a strong private sector to fill the gap. Where private traders have moved in to replace the state they have sometimes done so on highly unfavourable terms for poor farmers. In many instances, this left farmers more food insecure, and governments more reliant on unpredictable international aid flows.

While few would recommend a complete return to the interventionist policies of the past, many acknowledge the important role of the state in providing infrastructure and public goods to facilitate markets. The state also needs to set a legis-

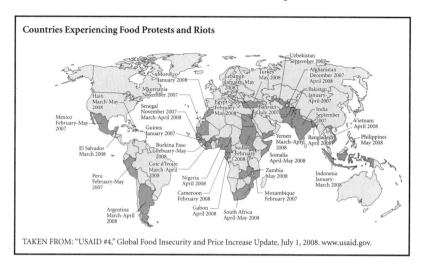

Countries Experiencing Food Protests and Riots

TAKEN FROM: "USAID #4," Global Food Insecurity and Price Increase Update, July 1, 2008. www.usaid.gov.

lative framework for land reform, and to provide technical assistance. There is now also growing recognition that direct state intervention—grain reserves to stabilise prices, cash transfers, or subsidised or free agricultural inputs—can provide a cheaper and more effective way of ensuring food security. The World Bank, for example, has recently acknowledged this in relation to government input schemes.

How Governments Should Intervene

The appropriate mix of interventions should be determined case by case in a consultative process between governments, civil society, and donors. Where markets are functioning, governments can provide cash transfers to help people buy agricultural inputs, as well as meet their immediate consumption needs. Another much-studied approach is the Malawian government's targeted-inputs programme, which consisted of a small pack of free inputs, including enough fertilizer for around 0.1 hectares, which was distributed widely to smallholders. There is evidence that this programme increased productivity and output of maize, and hence, income. However, this approach may not offer as much choice for farmers over inputs [such] as cash transfers. Another approach is targeted subsidies, though care must be taken to ensure that they are not captured by wealthier groups. Subsidising producers' organisations or co-operatives is another way of ensuring inputs and services to farmers and pastoralists, particularly if corruption precludes government intervention.

However, major efforts are needed to improve the quality of government intervention, and reduce the risks of political abuse and corruption. Also, both governments and donors need to move away from short-term politicized interventions and towards long-term, predictable strategies to support smallholders. According to a recent report on Malawi, donors' approaches in the agricultural sector have been characterised by short-term thinking, competitiveness, and personality politics, criticisms often made by donors about African governments. Because of donors' strong influence on government policy, this has contributed to inconsistent and contradictory agricultural policies that have seriously harmed the poor, and increased food insecurity.

> *"As politicians continue to raise the volume of the populist rhetoric on the campaign trail, we should remind ourselves that the government is not always best suited to tackle the issues of poverty and hunger."*

Government Should Not Be Responsible for Alleviating Malnutrition

Israel Ortega

Israel Ortega is a senior media services associate with the Heritage Foundation, a conservative think tank focusing on issues of national defense, economics, and limited government. In the following viewpoint, Ortega considers the role of federal government to address societal ills, arguing that churches and nonprofit groups are more effective in alleviating problems such as poverty, hunger, and homelessness than governmental programs are.

As you read, consider the following questions:

1. Which U.S. city went from having the nation's highest number of welfare recipients per capita to being a welfare success story in twenty years?

Israel Ortega, "Poverty and Hunger: Why the Government's Not the Answer," *The Heritage Foundation*, January 23, 2008. Reproduced by permission.

2. According to the author, how did President Bill Clinton's 1996 Welfare Reform Act fundamentally change the way the United States deals with poverty and welfare dependence?

3. How much money do nonprofit organizations contribute to the economy of Washington, D.C., every year, according to a joint study by the Nonprofit Roundtable of Greater Washington and the World Bank?

Thanks to the endless media coverage of the upcoming [2008] Presidential election, there is no shortage of candidates talking about the plight of Americans facing tough times. Many even say we have a moral obligation to help the poor and disenfranchised. Perhaps, but the real question may be: What is the appropriate role of the federal government?

As New Yorkers, we don't have to read statistics or listen to others talk about hunger and poverty. Unfortunately, for many of us, every day we see individuals panhandling in subways and on street corners. And yet as New Yorkers, we also understand better than most the difference between well-intentioned but flawed policy and actual proposals that will lift people out of poverty permanently.

It was, in fact, only twenty years ago that New York had the unfortunate distinction of having one of the nation's highest number of welfare recipients (per capita). Fast forward to today and New York is a true welfare success story. What's behind this remarkable turnaround?

1996 Welfare Reform Act

While the ink in the history books is not yet dry, the landmark 1996 Welfare Reform Act clearly deserves credit for the turnaround. Signed by former President Bill Clinton, the act fundamentally altered the way our country deals with welfare dependence and poverty. Essentially, the government stopped rewarding people for not working, while encouraging productivity.

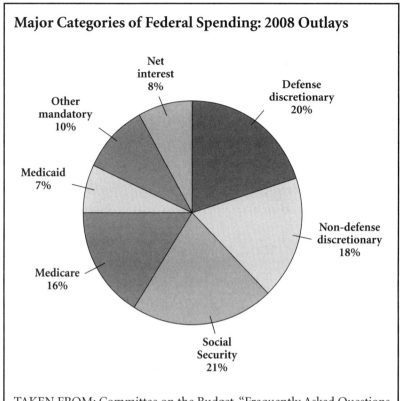

Major Categories of Federal Spending: 2008 Outlays

Net interest
8%

Defense discretionary
20%

Other mandatory
10%

Non-defense discretionary
18%

Medicaid
7%

Medicare
16%

Social Security
21%

TAKEN FROM: Committee on the Budget, "Frequently Asked Questions about the Federal Budget," U.S. House of Representatives, April 24, 2008. http://www.budget.house.gov.

It also emphasized that government programs had not demonstrated much success at helping the poor gain independence from welfare—that job was being better done by many community organizations around the country. Decried at the time by critics as heartless and mean, today the Welfare Reform Act is seen to be a clear success.

Of course the reality is that poverty persists and the question remains: What to do?

Government Not the Answer

Well, according to a recent study, the short answer may be—don't look to the government. According to a joint study conducted by the Nonprofit Roundtable of Greater Washington and the World Bank, nonprofit organizations contribute at least $9.6 billion to the Washington, D.C. region's economy. In short, the study describes how nonprofit groups have been more successful than the government in dealing with homelessness, hunger and violence.

Across the country, it's clear that churches and local nonprofits are filling the void for the government. In suburban Chicago, with its high concentration of Hispanic-Americans, the *Chicago Tribune* recently reported how the "Friend, I Shall Help" (FISH) food pantry is growing with volunteers and donations.

Locally, the St. Francis of Xavier Soup Kitchen in downtown Manhattan has been operating for decades helping to feed hungry New Yorkers.

As politicians continue to raise the volume of the populist rhetoric on the campaign trail, we should remind ourselves that the government is not always best suited to tackle the issues of poverty and hunger. Churches and nonprofits continue to lead the way in meeting these local needs, thanks in large part to the generosity of private citizens.

And so, as in so many things, the government is not the best answer.

> "The main role of the IGOs [interna-
> tional governmental organizations] is
> not to feed people directly but to help
> nations use their own resources more
> effectively."

International Governmental Organizations (IGOs) Should Help Alleviate Malnutrition

George Kent

George Kent is a professor at the University of Hawaii and the author of Freedom from Want: The Right to Adequate Food. *In the following viewpoint, he argues that international governmental organizations (IGOs) have an important role in alleviating hunger and malnutrition. Kent asserts that only with the help of IGOs can the doctrine of the "human right to adequate food" be fulfilled, because IGOs are in the unique position of being able to help nations utilize their resources more efficiently.*

As you read, consider the following questions:

1. What are the most prominent international governmental organizations (IGOs) that specialize in the areas of food and nutrition?

George Kent, *Food and Agriculture Organization of the United Nations*. Rome, Italy: 2003. Reproduced by permission.

2. What is the main function of a new global program for assuring realization of the human right to adequate food everywhere in the world?

3. What does the author envision a Global Nutrition Action Plan entailing?

What are—or should be—the obligations of the international community with regard to the human right to adequate food? How should the international community act to honor its obligations? Which agencies should have what duties? How can the international community, as a duty-bearer, be held accountable?

In advancing the human right to adequate food within nations, we know that it is wise to work with food and nutrition programs that are already in place. In many cases, the rules under which people have access to these programs could be revised to guarantee that those who are most needy are assured of receiving services. Similarly, instead of trying to invent something wholly new, use should be made of institutional arrangements that are already in place for dealing with food and nutrition issues at the global level. We should see how their methods of work can be adapted so that they help to carry out the obligations of the international community, and thus, help to advance the human right to adequate food globally.

The Top IGOs Dealing with Hunger and Malnutrition

The most prominent international governmental organizations (IGOs) concerned with food and nutrition are the Food and Agriculture Organization of the United Nations (FAO), the World Food Programme (WFP), the International Fund for Agricultural Development (IFAD), the World Health Organization (WHO), and the United Nations Children's Fund (UNICEF). They are governed by boards comprised of member states. Responsibility for coordinating food and nutrition activities among these and other IGOs in the United Nations system rests with the United Nations System Standing Committee on Nutrition, or SCN, formerly known as the United Nations Administrative Committee on Coordination/ Subcommittee on Nutrition. Representatives of bilateral donor agencies such as the Swedish International Development Agency (SIDA) and the United States Agency for International Development (USAID) also participate in SCN activities. The SCN also includes numerous international civil society organizations (ICSOs) concerned with food and nutrition.

Role of IGOs

The main role of the IGOs is not to feed people directly but to help nations use their own resources more effectively. In much the same way, recognition of the international dimensions of the human right to adequate food would not involve massive international transfers of food. The main function of a new global program for assuring realization of the human right to adequate food everywhere would be to press and help national governments address the problem of inadequate food among their own people, using resources within their own nations. There may always be a need for a global emergency food facility to help in emergency situations that are beyond the capacity of individual nations, but a different kind of design is needed for dealing with chronic food insecurity. Moreover, as chronic problems are addressed more effectively, nations would increase their capacity for dealing with emergency situations on their own. Over time, the need for emergency assistance from the outside would decline.

The IGOs could use their leverage to press for realization of the human right to adequate food within the nations they serve. For example, the World Food Programme could make it known that in providing food supplies for development it will favor those nations that are working to establish clear and effective entitlements for the most needy in their nations. The IGOs could be especially generous in providing assistance to those nations that create national laws and national agencies devoted to implementing the human right to adequate food. If they are relieved of some of the burden of providing material resources, poor nations might be more willing to create programs for recognizing and realizing the right. Such pledges by international agencies could be viewed as a precursor to recognition of a genuine international duty to recognize and effectively implement the human right to adequate food.

A Broad Agenda

The IGOs are concerned with the problems of famine and chronic malnutrition, but these are only a part of their broad agendas. For example, the FAO gives a great deal of attention to the interests of food producers, and WHO deals with the full range of health issues. UNICEF, too, addresses a very broad range of subjects. Malnutrition has not yet gotten the commitment of attention and resources needed to really solve the problem. The concept of moving progressively toward a global regime of a hard right to adequate food could be the basis for working out a global program of concerted action by the IGOs.

Launching a global human rights-based program for addressing widespread chronic malnutrition would require a global meeting in which all national governments and concerned international organizations were represented. They would have to make commitments and draw up action plans that are far stronger than those that have resulted in the past from other global meetings on food and nutrition.

Drawing up an Action Plan

What might the action plan look like? In some respects it would echo the *World Declaration on Nutrition* and the *Plan of Action for Nutrition* approved by the world's governments in Rome in December 1992. Certainly the early parts of those texts describing the nature of the problem and the seriousness of the governments' concerns would be similar. The big differences would be in the operational sections specifying who exactly is making what commitments to do what, in what time frame, with what sorts of accountability. The conference participants in 1992 went as far as they could go, but in the new agreement contemplated here we would look for a business-like contract, with clearly elaborated commitments.

At the 1992 meeting, the major parties were the nations of the world, and the concerned IGOs stood to the side as facilitators of the meeting. The focus was on the formulation of *national* plans of action, not a *global* plan of action. In the new negotiations envisioned here, the IGOs would be at center-stage, working out their roles in the global problem for the realization of the human right to adequate food. They would have to work out the division of responsibilities among them so that each could make its own best contribution to assuring that people were assured of adequate food. Of course, it would always have to be recognized that the IGOs are not independent agents, but are instruments of, and accountable to, their member nations.

Strategically, the program of action could begin the work of alleviating malnutrition with the very worst cases, and then as those problems were solved, move to dealing with less severe situations. Rules could be established so that the targets of action would be selected on the basis of clear measures of need, thus reducing the possibilities for making politicized selections. The IGOs could continue to carry out other functions, but with regard to the challenge of addressing serious malnutrition, their actions would be coordinated under the new global program of action, the contract adopted at the meeting.

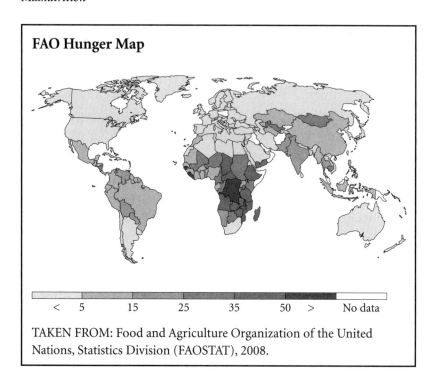

FAO Hunger Map

< 5 15 25 35 50 > No data

TAKEN FROM: Food and Agriculture Organization of the United Nations, Statistics Division (FAOSTAT), 2008.

The Global Nutrition Food Monitor

At the core of the new arrangement would be the establishment of a new global body—the Global Nutrition Program Monitor—that had responsibility for seeing to it that the terms of the contract—the Global Nutrition Action Plan—negotiated at the meeting were carried out. This new body, created by national governments working together with the IGOs, would see to it that those that made agreements, and thus incurred obligations, carried out their obligations in fact.

This Global Nutrition Program Monitor would not have substantive political power of its own, but would function in a manner comparable to that of the United Nations human rights treaty bodies. That is, through a process of constructive dialogue, it would call the parties to account for fulfilling the commitments they had agreed to make. The body would also serve in a coordinating role, and it would have the capacity to allocate resources provided to it.

The IGOs would support national governments in dealing with malnutrition among their own people. Local and international civil society organizations would be a part of the system in that they would help to identify and report serious cases of malnutrition, they would help to provide services, and they would monitor to make sure that national and local agencies carried out their work of alleviating malnutrition.

It would be agreed that where there was serious malnutrition and national agencies could not or would not solve the problem, the IGOs would have the authority and the duty to become directly involved. The nature of that involvement would have to be worked out. Concrete programs of action would have to be designed to fit particular cases, but the planning exercise would establish general procedures and guidelines for action. Consideration would have to be given to issues of consent, costs, logistics, risks, and so on. Intervention would not be automatic and indiscriminate, but there would be an agency in place that would be prepared to assess the situation and act under suitable internationally accepted guidelines. Initially, the international community would have a firm duty to assist only where there was consent from governments of the nations receiving assistance.

Earlier IGO Efforts

There have been comparable global planning efforts before. There were the *International Undertaking on World Food Security* of 1974, the *Plan of Action on World Food Security* of 1979, the *Agenda for Consultations and Possible Action to Deal with Acute and Large-scale Food Shortages* of 1981, and the *World Food Security Compact* of 1985. More recently, there was the *World Declaration and Plan of Action on Nutrition* formulated at the International Conference on Nutrition held in Rome in December 1992 and the comparable declaration and plan of action that emerged from the World Food Summit [WFS] of 1996, echoed again at the World Food Summit: five years later, held in 2002. This follow-up to the World Food Summit was delayed because of the events of September 11, 2001 [terrorist attacks on the United States].

The World Food Summit five years [2002] later did produce some movement with regard to the human right to adequate food. Paragraph 10 of the final *Declaration* called for the creation of an International Alliance Against Hunger, and in that context called upon the FAO Council to establish

> ... an Intergovernmental Working Group, with the participation of stakeholders, in the context of the WFS follow-up, to elaborate, in a period of two years, a set of voluntary guidelines to support Member States' efforts to achieve the progressive realisation of the right to adequate food in the context of national food security; we ask the FAO, in close collaboration with relevant treaty bodies, agencies and programmes of the UN System, to assist the Intergovernmental Working Group, which shall report on its work to the Committee on World Food Security.

This was a disappointment to many because the idea of voluntary guidelines replaced the idea of creating a code of conduct on the right to adequate food. This was a decisive move away from acknowledging any sort of firm obligation on the part of the international community with regard to the human right to adequate food. Norway explained its concern in this way:

> Norway would have preferred the expression code of conduct instead of voluntary guidelines because it is clearer and more definite. However, we hope that this will set in motion a process that will lead to a useful instrument that would have the same function as a code of conduct on the right to adequate food, and in fact lead to such a code in the future.

This contrasted sharply with the position taken by the United States on paragraph 10. . . .

How Plans Differ

The major differences between these earlier efforts and the Global Action Plan outlined here are the prominent roles of the international governmental organizations as actors, the sharply focused purpose and program of action, the clear contractual commitments, and most importantly, the creation of a central agency responsible for assuring that the commitments are honored. There would be a serious system of accountability at the global level.

Of course, the idea of ending serious malnutrition in the world through recognition of the human right to adequate food everywhere is idealistic. Nevertheless, the idea can be useful in setting the direction of action. We can think of the IGOs as having specific duties with regard to the fulfillment of the human right to adequate food. We can move progressively toward the ideal by inviting IGOs to establish clear rules and procedures that they would follow as if they were firm duties.

Strategic planning requires more than appointing committees and articulating goals. The sharp reduction (if not elimination) of malnutrition throughout the world will require clear articulation of the action required to achieve each particular target along the way, and clear commitment by the parties to take the actions that are required. If those parties are serious, they should be willing to create a body that would hold them to account for keeping those commitments.

> *"The issue of food security is too important to be left to politicians, national governments or the marketplace."*

Nongovernmental Organizations (NGOs) Should Help Alleviate Malnutrition

Anuradha Mittal

Anuradha Mittal is a contributor to Earth Island Journal, *in addition to being coordinator of the US section of FIAN and policy director at the Institute for Food and Development Policy. In the following viewpoint, Mittal argues that the free market cannot reduce the number of malnourished people in the world, and increasing international trade actually harms rather than helps the hunger problem. NGOs feel that food is a basic human right and governments need to provide that right to their citizens. Furthermore, the governments need to implement policies that involve the local people and lead to self-sufficiency. Mittal warns that if the battle over the right to food is lost, other basic human rights may follow.*

As you read, consider the following questions:

1. How many representatives were sent to the World Food Summit? How many countries did they represent?

Anuradha Mittal, "The Politics of Hunger," *Earth Island Journal*, vol. 12, Spring 1997, pp. 36–37. Copyright 1997 Earth Island Institute. Reproduced by permission.

2. What are the G77 countries and why was the group formed?

3. What action did the declaration that thousands of WFS delegates signed call for?

In 1974, the United Nations' first World Food Summit in Rome declared its intention to wipe out starvation within a decade. Twenty-three years later, the world is populated by 840 million chronically undernourished individuals.

Last November [1996], 1,200 representatives of farming, human rights and anti-hunger associations; women's organizations; and environmental groups from more than 80 countries assembled in Rome for the second World Food Summit (WFS) and Nongovernmental Organization (NGO) Forum, convened by the UN Food and Agriculture Organization (FAO). This time, bureaucrats and politicians declared their more modest intention to reduce by half the number of malnourished people within the next 18 years.

Unlike most nations, whose delegations included presidents, vice presidents and prime ministers, the US refused to send any of its top elected officials. The US also rejected the goal of the WFS's final declaration, which pledged to reduce the number of the world's hungry to 420 million by the year 2015. Delegates from the G77 countries (a group of Third World nations formed to counter the dominance of the world's seven industrialized countries) called the US performance "shameful."

The US rejected language guaranteeing the fundamental right to safe and nutritious food consistent with the right to be free from hunger. The US delegation maintained that this was "a goal or aspiration to be realized progressively, but [one that] does not give rise to any international obligations." Melinda Kimble, head of the US negotiating team, stated that an endorsement of the right to food would place new US welfare reform laws—mandating drastic cuts in food stamps and

Aid to Families with Dependent Children—in violation of international laws. Therefore, Kimble explained, the US could not sign the declaration.

Free Trade Reply to Hunger

The WFS's goal of merely halving the number of hungry humans has been shaped by a free market ideology that argues that the way to fight global hunger lies in deregulation, privatization and increased foreign investment. On the WFS's opening day, US Secretary of Agriculture Dan Glickman declared: "Domestic market reforms have unleashed the full potential of American agriculture. Our farmers now plant for world demand instead of for government programs."

What Glickman called "our farmers" are really the US-based transnational corporations that dominate global food production and commercialization. "Free and fair trade promotes global prosperity and plenty," Glickman proclaimed. "The private sector is the great untapped frontier in the world war on hunger." Driving the point home, the US insisted that "commitment four" of the Rome declaration be written to read: "We will strive to ensure that food, agricultural trade and overall trade policies are conducive to fostering food security for all through a fair and market-oriented world trade system." The objective is to strengthen the hegemony of the World Trade Organization (WTO) over the world's production and distribution of food.

World Bank President James D. Wolfensohn backed the US position with a call for governments to "reduce heavy intervention in the rural economy and concentrate on creating an economic regulatory environment that fosters agricultural growth."

Self-Sufficiency vs. Globalization

Glickman and Wolfensohn are advocates of a new global resolve to destroy the national self-sufficiency food systems set

Food Aid Deliveries in 2007 by Donor and Category

Donor	Total Food Aid	Food Aid Category		
		Emergency	Project	Programme
Total	**5,935,813**	**3,667,761**	**1,403,609**	**864,443**
Australia	127,853	76,291	51,562	
Canada	215,044	149,793	65,251	
China	307,147	297,315	1,931	7,900
Denmark	66,222	17,925	48,296	
European Commission	756,121	434,460	40,658	281,003
France	42,014	33,136	8,879	
Germany	144,086	54,981	89,106	
Ireland	47,874	47,027	847	
Italy	42,543	19,467	15,617	7,458
Japan	189,535	129,953	28,870	30,712
Korea, Republic of	431,432	31,432		400,000
Luxembourg	27,303	14,159	10,173	2,971
Netherlands	104,542	99,731	4,811	
Norway	81,390	30,912	50,477	
Russian Federation, the	28,603	23,736	4,867	
Spain	35,249	31,565	3,134	550
Sweden	73,503	73,125	378	
Switzerland	32,016	30,733	1,283	
UK	83,244	83,244		
USA	2,621,739	1,604,139	894,738	122,862
Intern. Gov. Org	35,485	35,485		
NGOs	68,563	31,141	37,422	
Others	138,855	92,509	35,358	10,988
UN	235,451	225,500	9,951	

TAKEN FROM: World Food Programme (WFP), *The Food Aid Monitor*, June 2008. http://www.wfp.org/interfais/index2.htm#.

up after World War II. Those systems were based on subsidies and tariff barriers designed to protect domestic producers, particularly in the US, western Europe and Japan. Communist countries created their own separate agricultural systems, while Third World countries such as Mexico, Brazil and India attempted to subsidize and protect their local producers.

The new international food regime has three central objectives: first, to remove national agricultural subsidies and protective tariffs in accordance with regional agreements like NAFTA and the Uruguay round of GATT (General Agreement on Tariffs and Trade); second, to promote a greater role for transnational capital in food provisioning systems worldwide under the guise of free trade; and finally, to demolish national economies in the Third World and the former Soviet bloc under the auspices of structural adjustment programs.

These policy changes are contributing to a new export-oriented emphasis in agriculture and the unprecedented escalation of economic inequalities within and between countries and regions.

In response to the WFS's official trade-based plan of action, NGO representatives maintained that policies must be shifted to ensure that food security through self-sufficiency takes priority over world market integration.

The NGO statement, "Profit for Few or Food For All," saw food as a basic human right that national governments—not the market—have the responsibility to provide. The statement went on to indict globalization and the lack of transnational corporate accountability as chief causes of increased world poverty.

The NGOs were struck by one spurious argument at the core of all of the official documents—the assertion that the way to achieve food security is not by helping farmers to grow more food for local markets, but rather by boosting international trade.

Three interrelated assumptions show the hollowness of the FAO's trade policies.

More Trade = More Food?

The FAO documents state:

Trade has a major bearing on access to food via its positive effect on economic growth, incomes and employment. . . . Without trade, people and countries would have to rely exclusively on their own production: Average income would be far lower, the choice of goods would be far less and hunger would increase.

A look at India proves otherwise. During the last five years of trade liberalization, agricultural exports increased by more than 70 percent. At the same time, domestic food prices increased by at least 63 percent. A survey by India's National Institute of Nutrition shows that the average daily per capita consumption of cereals has dropped by 14 grams per person since the late 1980s.

The Indian government is pushing exports, while denying ration cards to poor people and cutting family food quotas. Large segments of India's population are at the mercy of the open market's skyrocketing prices. Free trade has not led to increased food security.

Market Gains Trickle Away

The FAO argues that increased trade raises overall income, which "trickles down" to each household.

In 1987, in India, 361 million people lived in abject poverty. Today, the proportion of households below the poverty line has increased in both rural and urban areas.

In the 200 million-strong Indian middle class, lower-end incomes are dropping off, while upper-end incomes are increasing dramatically. If anything, free trade has caused benefits to trickle up.

Higher Income = Food Security?

The third FAO assumption—that increasing household income will lead to greater food security—is made even as the FAO document acknowledges that the trickle-down approach may make matters worse for farmers and peasants:

Because small-scale producers often lack the resources necessary to grow export-oriented crops . . . they may find that commercial expansion has an inflationary effect on production costs and on land rent that may even make their traditional production less feasible. Small producers may abandon their land or be bought out by larger commercial interests . . . and export agriculture may worsen the position of the poor majority.

According to government estimates, some 2 million small and marginal Indian farmers lose their subsidies or even their land each year. Putting India's food security in the hands of a few giant agribusinesses—while the poor are landless and unemployed—is a sure recipe for famine. Land loss will become more common as new farm policies further relax rural landholding laws for businesses.

For almost a decade, the goal of national and international food and farm policies has been to lower consumer food prices by increasing food imports. Trade liberalization has kept farm prices in most countries at below-cost-of-production levels, putting many farmers (both in major exporting countries and importing countries) out of business.

The US government currently plans to make more aggressive use of trade negotiations to dismantle foreign import tariffs, import quotas, production subsidies and other "trade barriers" to build food import demand abroad and fuel agricultural export growth.

US dumping of underpriced grain surpluses has destroyed poor farmers in many food-importing countries. In 1965, the US unloaded grain in India in the name of "food aid," driving down the price of domestic wheat and curtailing native production. Over the past few years, the Mexican government put 1.8 million corn farmers out of business by choosing to import heavily subsidized corn from the US.

Rock-bottom world corn prices (set by the US) averaging about half the cost of production have encouraged cattle farmers to concentrate on confined livestock operations (where cattle eat grain that otherwise would be used for human consumption). Low grain prices have made corn sweeteners so cheap that Pepsi and Coca-Cola have abandoned cane and beet sugar in favor of corn syrup, driving world sugar prices to all-time lows and cutting into the foreign exchange earnings of many Third World countries.

Ill-Founded Green Revolutions

New WTO agricultural trade rules may lead to more effective food embargoes as they result in the elimination of national food storage programs. US doubling of export prices for basic grains in the summer of 1996 was essentially an embargo against the poor countries that most needed these supplies.

Most governments still see hunger as a problem of production shortfall. The US, for example, argued that the solution to hunger lies in more intensive use of biotechnology, pesticides, artificial fertilizers, irrigation and greater freedom for transnational food corporations. While countries like India still are taking stock of the socioeconomic and environmental costs of Green Revolution I (the introduction of hybrid crops, chemical fertilizers and pesticides from the mid-60s to the mid-80s), the FAO has found it opportune to launch Green Revolution II, betting the world's food future on the promise of genetic engineering (with all the corresponding environmental safeguards, of course).

The NGOs insisted that any revolution, green or otherwise, must be undertaken in partnership with the peasants and the local society.

A Century of Food Rebellions?

Since the 1976 mass demonstrations in Peru in response to food price increases imposed by the International Monetary Fund (IMF), riots and protests have taken place in dozens of countries.

In 1994, the Zapatistas burst forth in Chiapas, Mexico, demanding land, food and an adequate standard of living. Food shortages fostered by drought, peso devaluation and the impact of NAFTA and GATT on peasant farmers have driven bands of women and children to rob grain trains.

In July 1996, protests forced the Jordanian government to abandon IMF-imposed plans to triple the price of bread. Last September, Argentines rose up against government plans to increase the cost of food and other basic amenities by 10-46 percent.

Last October [1996], Bolivian labor unions called a general strike after tens of thousands of peasants camped out in La Paz to protest government plans to expropriate their land and sell it to agribusiness. Similar protests have rocked Kazakhstan, Pakistan and Bulgaria.

The current period of widespread protest against hunger and austerity measures is reminiscent of a similar period in the late 18th century in western Europe. The French Revolution was driven not only by demands for political freedom, but also by the lack of bread in Paris. Food riots have occurred throughout the history of market societies, whenever government policies caused severe economic hardship, betrayed the moral basis of society and clashed with the basic human right to food.

For most of the Third World, trade liberalization really means neocolonialism and a hegemonic worldwide capitalist system, represented largely by the US and a few other powers.

During the WFS, Cuban President Fidel Castro was one of the few world leaders to challenge participants to look squarely at reality. "Hunger," he said, "is the offspring of injustice and the unequal distribution of the wealth in this world. . . . What kind of magical solutions are we going to provide so that in 20 years from now there will be 400 million instead of 800 million starving people? . . . Let the truth prevail, and not hypocrisy and deceit."

Despite US intransigence, there was consensus among governments and NGOs for making "the human right to food" the summit's chief demand and commitment. In the official plan of action, the UN commissioner for human rights was given the task of pulling together global agencies to ensure implementation of the right to food. In his speech to the NGO forum, the chair of the FAO's Food Security Committee, Chile's ambassador to the FAO, vowed to take this concept to all of the important UN forums.

Thousands of WFS delegates from more than 50 countries signed an NGO declaration calling for the creation of "effective instruments to implement the right to food. These instruments should include a code of conduct to govern the activities of those involved in achieving the right to food, including national and international institutions, as well as private actors, such as transnational corporations."

The WFS made it clear that the issue of food security is too important to be left to politicians, national governments or the marketplace. The transition to a restorative, sustaining democracy requires profound changes in our values and the way we understand human rights. The time has come to make freedom from hunger a reality. If we fail to exercise this right, we may lose other human rights as well.

"It is in . . . examples of productive partnerships between government and civil society organizations that local inspiration and creativity are found to solve the global problems of poverty. NGOs [non-governmental organizations] and other civil society organizations thus help Governments and peoples to energize the process to achieve the MDGs [Millennium Development Goals] by 2015, and thus to halve poverty."

Global Partnerships Can Contribute to the Fight Against Malnutrition

Liesbeth Venetiaan-Vanenburg

Liesbeth Venetiaan-Vanenburg is the first lady of the Republic of Suriname, located in northern South America. In the following viewpoint, she emphasizes the importance of forming partnerships to eradicate hunger and malnutrition through a focus on eradicating its root cause—poverty. She finds education to be key in this effort, and urges a thorough consideration of all aspects of

Liesbeth Venetiaan-Vanenburg, "Eradication of Poverty and Hunger through Global Partnership for Development," *Global Watch*, Summer 2007. Copyright Millennium Development Goal Global Watch Summer 2007. Reproduced by permission.

poverty in order to understand and defeat it. She also recognizes that global partnerships are vital in the fight against hunger, malnutrition, and poverty.

As you read, consider the following questions:

1. What does the author consider the important first step in eradicating poverty, hunger, and malnutrition all over the world?
2. Why is education key in the fight against poverty, hunger, and malnutrition, according to the author?
3. How do partnerships between governments, non-governmental organizations (NGOs), international governmental organizations (IGOs), and other civil society organizations work together to alleviate poverty, hunger, and malnutrition?

Poverty and hunger are violations of fundamental human rights and a serious infringement of the security of human beings. Poverty makes it impossible for people to ensure for themselves and their dependents a set of basic minimum conditions required for their subsistence and well-being. And in their countless manifestations, poverty and hunger continue to be serious obstacles and threats to development.

When we, mothers, talk about poverty and hunger, we look first and foremost at our children and our families, whom we are unable to feed. We cry because we cannot provide for them, yet it is also the image of our children and families that strengthen our determination to fight poverty, to seek ways to feed our families, and to urge them on to a better way of life.

Eradicating Poverty Is Vital

During the meeting of "America's Youth Voice" in Santo Domingo in 2003, participants defined poverty, listed causes, and identified the need to eradicate poverty. They described poverty "as the lack of access to, or control over sufficient resources, including land, skills, knowledge, connections necessary to ensure adequate access to acceptable levels and quality of income, health and knowledge for living".

Too many people still accept poverty and hunger as grim and inevitable facts of life. Young people become frustrated, because they endure the economic situation of their parents without feeling that they themselves will be able to change anything. This need not be the case. Hunger and malnutrition cannot and should not be inevitable results in a world of plenty.

But how can we end poverty, hunger and malnutrition in our countries? Where do we start? There are no simple answers, but there are common approaches that have proven to be effective in accelerating the process.

The First Step in Eliminating Poverty

As a fundamental first step, the elimination of poverty, including hunger and malnutrition, must be adopted as a primary goal of national, social and economic development.

Breaking the cycle of poverty is not merely undertaking one action or setting out to achieve one target. We must look at all characteristics and aspects of poverty, and try to tackle the issues holistically and integrally. This is what the Millennium Development Goals [MDGs] have set out to do. Focusing on attaining only one of the MDGs will not help us to eradicate poverty and hunger.

Yet, as we commence this forum and our discussions on the MDGs, I would nevertheless like to emphasize the importance of good education as one of the most important facets of poverty eradication, and one that is often underestimated and sometimes disregarded.

Education Is Important

Education is not only the key to learning in school or training for a good job; it is the key to attaining more justice in this world. For, education is vital to enhancing people's independence, it creates better opportunities for them to eliminate marginalization and strengthens their self-esteem. Education is an important instrument for people to attain self-respect, improve family life, build the necessary capacity and skills to survive and develop optimally, acquire specific knowledge, become technologically literate, and I could go on and on, adding to my list of why a good education is a prerequisite for every human being to be able to survive in this constantly and rapidly changing world. Early childhood education and good parenting provide the basic conditions for the empowerment and development of all people, and the cycle of good education never ends.

In Suriname [a country in northern South America], Government and civil society organizations have always taken education seriously. General and cultural education are both emphasized in national policy as important instruments to combat poverty and guide people towards achieving sustainable human development. Cultural education is regarded as important in Suriname because of the multi-ethnic and multi-religious population. It envisions that people who know their identity, their culture and their history, and who have knowledge of and respect for one another's cultures, will become strong and able to perform optimally.

Our "National Education Plan", which is now being implemented, emphasizes the need for good education for people to fend for themselves and grow into individuals with human dignity. The plan puts special emphasis on vulnerable groups, such as boys who do not complete their basic education and then tend to enter into criminal illegal environments. Other areas of focus are the education of children and youngsters living in remote areas, in Suriname primarily the indigenous and maroon children of the interior, and youngsters and adults who may have dropped out of the education system and require special training to further develop their potential.

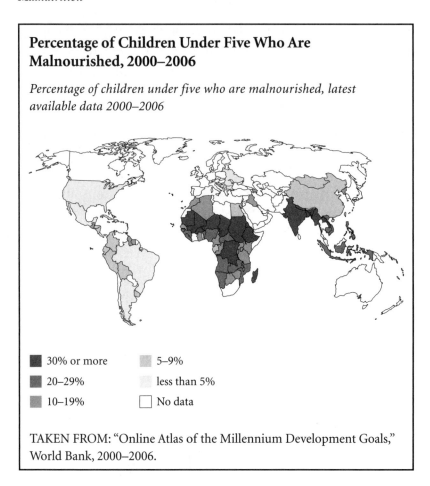

Percentage of Children Under Five Who Are Malnourished, 2000–2006

Percentage of children under five who are malnourished, latest available data 2000–2006

- ■ 30% or more
- ■ 20–29%
- ■ 10–19%
- ■ 5–9%
- ☐ less than 5%
- ☐ No data

TAKEN FROM: "Online Atlas of the Millennium Development Goals," World Bank, 2000–2006.

Partnerships Are Key

We are all aware that civil society organizations and the Government need to operate in close collaboration in order to achieve the MDGs. In Suriname, civil society organizations play an important part in providing good education and development opportunities for youngsters and adults alike in a variety of ways, in both formal and informal contexts, and their share in school renovation programs is crucial.

It is in such examples of productive partnerships between Government and civil society organizations that local inspiration and creativity are found to solve the global problems of poverty. NGOs [non-governmental organizations] and other civil society organizations thus help Governments and peoples to energize the process to achieve the MDGs by 2015, and thus to halve poverty.

Civil society organizations are indispensable in the process of achieving the MDGs, because they work directly with the people and have proven that they can apply a wide range of poverty reduction strategies, including strategies to enhance and widen initiatives for good education for all. People are never too poor, too young, too old, too weak, too disabled, or not educated enough, to organize themselves to improve their lives and to fight against poverty and hunger. NGOs often ensure that the voices of these vulnerable groups in society are heard: the youth, senior citizens, the disabled, people living in remote areas. They are catalysts for creative thought and action, and can bridge the way to policy makers, making sure that feasible ideas find their way into policy documents designed to eradicate poverty and hunger, and promote sustainable development.

Periodical Bibliography

The following articles have been selected to supplement the diverse views presented in this chapter.

Leslie Berliant — "Agricultural Research Funds Dry Up as World Hunger Reemerges," *Celsias*, June 20, 2008.

Kevin Clarke — "No More CARE Packages," *U.S. Catholic*, November 2007.

Trevalyn Garner Gruber — "Feeding Africa," *New Scientist*, July 3, 2004.

"'Fixing' Hunger in the 21st Century: How Food Sovereignty Might Turn Agriculture 'Right-Side Up'," *Appetite*, November 2006.

Tony Hall — "A Mandate for Action," *Sojourners Magazine*, July 2008.

Francis Moore Lappé — "The Shortage Isn't Food, It's Democracy," *Sojourners Magazine*, July 2008.

Eric Pape — "The 'Hunger Season,'" *Newsweek*, August 15, 2005.

Avi Salzman — "A Crisis in Global Food Aid," July 9, 2008. www.businessweek.com.

Avi Salzman — "U.S. Food Aid: We Pay for Shipping," July 10, 2008. www.businessweek.com.

Hazel Smith — "Gobbledygook," *World Today*, February 2003.

Sahra Sulaiman — "Agents of Transformation and Emancipation?: Relief NGOs, the Framing of Emergencies, and the Implications for the Changing Structures of Global Governance," *Conference Papers—International Studies Association*, 2007.

Armstrong Williams — "We Need a New Coalition of the Willing," *New Statesman*, July 14, 2003. "Ending Poverty," *New York Amsterdam News*, March 22, 2007.

OPPOSING
VIEWPOINTS®
SERIES

CHAPTER 4

What Policies Will
Alleviate Malnutrition?

Chapter Preface

For centuries, when populations were faced with drought or conflict that disrupted their food supplies, they were forced to move to an area in which they could find food or work. Food aid also became a way to help those in need; those who had food shared with those who did not. Until the age of the photograph, however, people were only able to hear about these emergency food crises by newspaper reports or accounts from eyewitnesses. In this modern age, people in the United States can see the effects of a tsunami in Indonesia or a government-approved genocide campaign in Darfur in real time, on the Internet or on their televisions.

Bringing the reality of humanitarian crises into the homes of citizens all over the world has in some cases increased the pressure to successfully address the issue. Seeing the suffering of innocent young children as they struggle against the ravages of hunger and malnutrition has redoubled the efforts of humanitarian groups to address the problem. Several promising breakthroughs in the fight against global malnutrition have emerged in the past few years. Probably one of the most promising is the creation of Plumpy'nut.

Scientists have been developing ready-to-use food (RUF) for years, especially forms of powdered milk that gives malnourished children vitamins and minerals they need to develop and flourish. However, most impoverished areas do not have access to clean water to mix with the powder and no access to refrigeration. In 1999, French pediatric nutritionist André Briend found an alternative to powdered milk by inventing the formula for Plumpy'nut.

Plumpy'nut is a high-protein, high-energy paste made from peanuts that comes in a foil wrapper. It requires no preparation; an individual can open the package and begin eating immediately. It travels well, needs no refrigeration, and has a shelf life of more than two years, which makes it easy to deploy in isolated areas and under difficult conditions. It provides essential vitamins (A, B-complex, C, D, E and K) and minerals (calcium, phosphorus, potassium, magnesium, zinc, copper, iron, iodine, sodium, and selenium), is rich in protein, and is 500 calories per pouch.

Used in extreme malnutrition crises, such as in Niger and Darfur, Plumpy'nut has proven to be extremely successful. Humanitarian aid workers provide two packages of Plumpy'nut to a malnourished child a day, and the results have been impressive. In Darfur, 30,000 severely malnourished children were given Plumpy'nut, and aid workers reported that it cut the malnutrition rates in half. In 2005, humanitarian aid workers deployed Plumpy'nut to the most malnourished areas in Niger, and lowered the rate of malnutrition dramatically.

Today Plumpy'nut treats approximately 120,000 children in the areas hit worst by malnutrition. It is relatively inexpensive to produce, and costs $1 for a day's worth per child. It promises to be a go-to solution to alleviate severe malnutrition in some of the most difficult areas in the world, and may be one of several ways to address the problem, along with many other solutions discussed in the following chapter.

"A new strategy of delivering essential nutrients through simple, highly nutritious ready-to-use food (RUF), specifically designed for young children, has greatly expanded the potential for effective nutritional interventions."

Nutrition Intervention Will Help Alleviate Malnutrition

Doctors Without Borders

Doctors Without Borders/Médecins Sans Frontières (MSF) is an international medical humanitarian organization that provides aid in nearly sixty countries to people whose survival is threatened by violence, negligence, or catastrophe, primarily due to armed conflict, epidemics, malnutrition, or natural disasters. In the following viewpoint, the organization encourages the growing trend toward nutrition intervention through ready-to-use-food (RUF), claiming that it is the only way to assure the nutrient security of young children at risk of malnutrition.

As you read, consider the following questions:

1. What are the benefits of ready-to-use-food (RUF), according to the viewpoint?
2. According to World Health Organization (WHO) estimates, how many children around the world are suffering from acute malnutrition?
3. How many calories and essential nutrients does each RUF packet provide to a malnourished child?

Persistent high rates of child mortality in sub-Saharan Africa and Asia will not be reduced if malnutrition is not addressed more aggressively. This is a medical emergency.

MSF [Médecins Sans Frontières—Doctors Without Borders] teams see the devastating impact of childhood malnutrition every day, having treated more than 150,000 children in ninety-nine programmes in 2006. Malnutrition weakens resistance and increases the risk of dying from pneumonia, diarrhoea, malaria, measles and AIDS, five diseases that are responsible for half of all deaths in children under five.

Despite its overwhelming contribution to child mortality and its impact on long-term health, treatment of malnutrition has not been a high enough priority in international and national public health planning and programming.

Current policies to address malnutrition have serious flaws. Many programmes designed to reduce mortality of young children from malnutrition focus on changing behaviours of mothers, education about proper food choices, and addressing poverty or food security.

Such strategies are insufficient because mothers in the Sahel, the Horn of Africa or Asia don't just need advice about how to feed their children. They need access to foods that contain the forty essential nutrients a young child, particularly under the age of three, needs to grow and be healthy. Exclusive breastfeeding, which is widely promoted, is only enough to meet the nutritional needs until six months of age.

Ready-to-Use Food (RUF)

Addressing the long-term challenges of poverty and food security is equally important but is not enough to address the
needs of malnourished children that are at greatest risk of dying today.

A new strategy of delivering essential nutrients through
simple, highly nutritious ready-to-use food (RUF), specifically
designed for young children, has greatly expanded the potential for effective nutritional interventions.

The vast majority of seriously malnourished children can
now receive treatment at home, under the supervision of their
mother or other caregiver, instead of in hospital.

Despite accumulated evidence of therapeutic RUF's effectiveness—high cure rates, low mortality and low default
rates—donors and UN agencies continue to ship hundreds of
thousands of tons of fortified blended flours to be distributed
as supplementary foods, even when the effectiveness of this
strategy has proven to be limited for children under the age of
three.

Reasons for Malnutrition

Children become malnourished when they do not receive the
adequate nutrients their bodies require to resist infection and
maintain growth. When nutritional deficiencies become too
significant, a child will begin to 'waste'—to consume his/her
own tissues to obtain needed nutrients. Wasting is a sign of
acute malnutrition.

In some regions of the world, such as in Africa's Sahel,
wasting is particularly frequent among children during the
'hunger gap' period, between harvests. The World Health Organization (WHO) estimates that there are 20 million young
children with severe acute malnutrition at any given point in
time.

However, only about 3 percent of children with severe
acute malnutrition have access to therapeutic RUF.

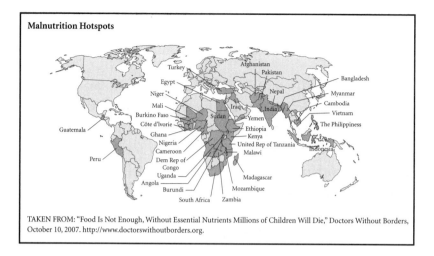

Malnutrition Hotspots

TAKEN FROM: "Food Is Not Enough, Without Essential Nutrients Millions of Children Will Die," Doctors Without Borders, October 10, 2007. http://www.doctorswithoutborders.org.

Nutritional Needs of a Growing Child

A World Health Organization (WHO) multi-country study leading to the development of the WHO Child Growth Standards (2006) has shown that all children across all regions can attain a similar standard of height and weight and development with optimal nutrition, good health care and a healthy environment. Therefore, the nutritional needs of rapidly growing children everywhere in the world are essentially the same.

Breast milk is the only food that a child younger than six months of age needs. After six months, children require more energy and essential nutrients than breast milk alone can provide. This includes proteins and essential fats, as well as vitamins and minerals such as calcium, potassium, zinc and iron.

How Needs Are Met in Developed Countries

In developed countries, young children eat a variety of nutrient-dense foods such as meat, poultry, fish and eggs, as well as fruits and vegetables to meet their nutritional requirements, as they continue to breastfeed. Even if infants don't eat meat, infant foods and cereals are fortified with vitamins and minerals, especially iron and zinc, in order to meet their nutritional needs.

Milk is a good source of most of these nutrients (except iron) and is an important part of most children's diets after one year of age.

In resource-limited settings, diets consist primarily of plant-source foods, with little added fat. These lack iron, zinc, and calcium in particular and nutrients are not as easily absorbed from plant foods as they are from meats, fish, poultry, eggs, or dairy. However, these animal-source foods are usually prohibitively expensive or simply not available.

Limitations of Fortified Blended Foods

Corn soy blend (CSB) and other fortified blended foods have long been used in food assistance programmes to prevent nutrient deficiencies. The composition has remained largely unchanged despite better knowledge about how to best meet the nutritional needs of young children.

Animal (dairy) protein is best suited to maximizing growth of young children. The composition of CSB, being an exclusively plant-based food without any dairy component, is not ideal to facilitate growth of children in the first two years of life.

CSB also contains a number of elements that limit the body's ability to absorb the nutrients that are present. Additionally, preparing CSB requires clean water, which is often not available in resource-limited settings, time for cooking, and also bears the risk of being over-diluted.

Why Does Ready-to-Use Food Work?

Experience by different organisations including MSF has shown that a very successful way to deliver essential nutrients to malnourished children is with ready-to-use food (RUF). This is an effective treatment because each packet delivers 500 calories in the form of a dense nutrient spread that contains milk powder and the forty essential nutrients that a malnour-ished child needs to replete nutrient deficiencies and gain weight.

Further, RUF is simple to use in resource-limited settings as an efficient and safe way to provide milk to children under the age of three: it contains no water, making it resistant to bacterial contamination; it comes in individually wrapped air-tight foil packets; no preparation is required; the product has a long shelf life; and it is easy to transport and use in hot climates.

Most critically, the vast majority of malnourished children can take this treatment at home, under the supervision of their mother or caregiver, instead of in hospital. This allows programmes to reach many more children, while at the same time minimising the risk for children of contracting an infection in hospital.

Malnutrition must be addressed before it reaches a life-threatening stage. The quality of complementary foods provided to children after six months of age in resource-limited settings requires re-examining. If any of the forty essential nutrients are deficient in a young child's diet, the body's defences are weakened and the likelihood of falling seriously ill from a minor infection increases.

| "*Despite their contributions to the global food supply, women farmers are often undervalued and overlooked in agricultural development strategies.*"

Empowering Women Will Help Alleviate Malnutrition

Laura Johnston Monchuk

Laura Johnston Monchuk is a contributor to the Canadian Federation of Agriculture, an advocacy group representing more than 200,000 Canadian farm families. The association promotes Canadian agriculture and food producers in Canada and abroad. In the following viewpoint, Monchuk outlines the key role women farmers play in food production all over the world. She describes the inequality women farmers face, particularly when it comes to access to resources, and argues that women should be active participants in the formulation of global agricultural development strategies.

As you read, consider the following questions:

1. According to United Nations' Food and Agriculture Organization (FAO) estimates, women are responsible for how much of the world's food production?

Laura Johnston Monchuk, "Empowering Women Farmers Is Key to Rural Vitality," *Canadian Federation of Agriculture*, December 12, 2006. Reproduced by permission.

2. What percentage of the food supply in Africa is produced by women?

3. If women were given equal access to resources, what
   effect would that have on agricultural productivity, according to the International Food Policy Research Institute?

The United Nations' Food and Agriculture Organization
(FAO) estimates that women are responsible for half of
the world's food production. Despite their contributions to
the global food supply, women farmers are often undervalued
and overlooked in agricultural development strategies.

Vital Role of Female Farmers

"In the poorest countries, rural women produce a very large
proportion of the food," said Karen Serres, a French farmer
and president of the International Federation of Agricultural
Producers (IFAP) Committee on Women in Agriculture. "Hunger and malnutrition still concern too many countries, and
women farmers are right on the front line in fighting these
problems. However, female farmers are largely under-
represented in every continent in the world."

In Asian countries, women produce approximately 60 percent of the food; and women produce more than 80 percent
of the food in Africa. In these and other regions, women are
often restricted from owning or inheriting the land they use,
which excludes them from accessing credit. Across the developing world, studies have shown that women find it more difficult than men to gain access to land, credit, seeds, tools, education, technology, training and basic human rights.

According to the FAO, the majority of the world's poor
live in rural areas, and 70 percent of the rural poor are women
whose principal resource is agriculture. A study for the International Food Policy Research Institute points out if women

farmers were given equal access to resources, developing countries would see significant increases in agricultural productivity.

Women Farmers in Canada

In Canada, rural life continues to change and women are bearing much of the responsibility of rural economic transformation, according to Prof. Belinda Leach, holder of the University of Guelph Research Chair in Rural Gender Studies. "Rural women are simultaneously dealing with disappearing social services, declining farm incomes and fewer employment and schooling options," she said. "Many hold down full-time jobs, both on and off the farm, while continuing to be the primary caregivers of children and elderly relatives."

According to the 2001 Canadian Census of Agriculture, 26 percent of Canada's 346,200 farm operators are female. Mostly, they work on two-operator farms where the other operator is male, likely a spouse. While the proportion of all Canadian farms operated exclusively by men is large—64 percent—it has decreased in the last ten years. While still small, the proportion of farms operated exclusively by women has grown from 3.9 percent a decade ago, to 5 percent in 2001.

"In Canada and abroad, women are the backbone of rural communities, working diligently both on and off the farm," said Erna Ference, Alberta chicken farmer and Canadian Federation of Agriculture board member. "Rural Canadian women play multiple roles that are key to maintaining our farms, our families and our communities. It is important that rural women are also active participants in the creation of global agricultural development strategies."

Developing Strategies to Empower Women

Cultural barriers and limited finances, time and information often deter women from participating in recognized leadership positions, particularly in developing countries. The de-

Share of Women in Total Employment by Job Status 1990–2005 (Percentage)

Wage employment in most of Africa and in many parts of Asia and Latin America is concentrated in urban areas. Outside cities and towns, most employment is in agriculture, and mainly for family subsistence. Women in developing regions are more likely than men to work in agriculture, and as contributing but unpaid family workers. Worldwide, over 60 percent of unpaid family workers are women—meaning that women continue to lack access to job security and social protection.

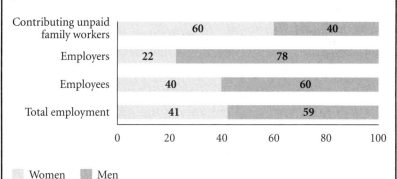

TAKEN FROM: The Millennium Development Goals Report, United Nations 2007. www.un.org.

valuation of women's role in agriculture also leads to unequal influence in policy-making in various regions of the world. IFAP and its member organizations have developed strategies for governments, farm organizations, and rural women to help overcome obstacles to female rural leadership. Such strategies are opening doors for a growing number of rural women in developing countries to participate in producer groups and cooperative ventures and to gain better control of their economic destinies.

"Crisis has provided us opportunity," explained Nibia Olid, president of the Asociacion de Mujeres Rurales des Uruguay (AMRU) and vice chair of the IFAP Women's Committee. Her organization has provided a platform for rural Uruguayan women to obtain technical training, leadership formation, and small business development. More than 1,800 women from 180 groups have united through AMRU to increase their incomes and improve the quality of life of their families and communities. Marketing under the common brand, "Delicias Criollas," these women have entered the growing organic niche market by providing all-natural homemade food products.

"Before they can represent societal interests in leadership positions, rural women on all continents must be recognized as leaders, not only by society, but also by themselves," Serres said. "A greater participation of women in leadership positions could strengthen economies, accelerate development, and improve social programs, resulting in increased benefits for all."

"Empowering female farmers worldwide is important to ending world hunger and enhancing the quality of life among rural populations," said Canadian Federation of Agriculture President Bob Friesen. "As a member of the International Federation of Agricultural Producers, CFA is working alongside farm groups from other countries to help reduce poverty and empower farmers globally. Our members are well-equipped and committed to sharing expertise and knowledge with developing countries on systems and structures that provide a strong voice for their fellow farmers."

> *"The changing interaction between agriculture and nutrition in a globalizing and urbanizing world demands new policy responses: old lessons need to be applied and adapted to new realities; emerging challenges and opportunities must be recognized and addressed."*

Implementing Effective Agricultural Trade Policies Will Help Alleviate Malnutrition

Corinna Hawkes and Marie T. Ruel

Corinna Hawkes is a research fellow in the Food Consumption and Nutrition Division (FCND) at the International Food Policy Research Institute (IFPRI), and Marie T. Ruel is director of FCND at IFPRI. In the following viewpoint, they outline the ways in which growing globalization and urbanization have impacted agricultural policy over the past few decades, arguing that new responses are imperative to prevent and alleviate problems of undernutrition and obesity.

Corinna Hawkes and Marie T. Ruel, *Focus 13: Understanding the Links Between Agriculture and Health*. Washington, DC: International Food Policy Research Institute, 2006. Copyright © 2006 International Food Policy Research Institute. All rights reserved. Reproduced by permission of the International Food Policy Research Institute www.ifpri. org.

As you read, consider the following questions:

1. What are the four lessons the agricultural sector learned when it came to addressing undernutrition, according to the authors?

2. How have globalization and urbanization seriously impacted the agricultural sector and how it addresses undernutrition?

3. According to the authors, what have rising populations, urbanization, and growing incomes meant to the agricultural sector in China the past few years?

Agriculture is fundamental to achieving nutrition goals: It produces the food, energy, and nutrients essential for human health and well-being. Gains in food production have played a key role in feeding growing and malnourished populations. Yet they have not translated into a hunger-free world nor prevented the development of further nutritional challenges. Micronutrient deficiencies (for example, of vitamin A, iron, iodine, and zinc) are now recognized as being even more limiting for human growth, development, health, and productivity than energy deficits. Hunger among the poor also increasingly manifests itself through excessive consumption of energy-rich but nutrient-poor foods. The result is a double burden of undernutrition (deficiencies of energy, micronutrients, or both) and "overnutrition" (poor diet quality leading to obesity and other diet-related chronic illnesses).

Lessons from the Past

Agriculture is often viewed as a predominantly economic activity. But in the 1960s and 1970s, concerns about food shortages and growing populations led to an increased focus among policy makers, researchers, and donor agencies on maximizing agriculture's nutritional potential. These efforts initially focused on staple food production and the generation of income among agricultural households and, in later decades, took account of the key role of micronutrient-rich foods and women to good nutrition. The experiences provide some key lessons on how the agricultural sector can help address undernutrition:

1. *Increasing the availability and affordability of staple foods.* In the 1960s and 1970s, governments made major investments in increasing the yields of staple food crops. In this Green Revolution, farmers' adoption of high-yielding varieties increased cereal availability by nearly 30 percent per person in South Asia and reduced the price of wheat and rice globally. But production gains did not automatically translate into equally large nutritional gains, since staples lack several essential micronutrients needed for child nutrition, and households could not necessarily access and afford the increased food supply.

2. *Raising incomes in households engaged in agricultural work.* Higher incomes increase households' ability to gain access to food, an especially important concern for poor agricultural households at risk from undernutrition. In the 1970s and 1980s, as agriculture became more commercialized in many developing countries, research found that new agricultural strategies, such as cash cropping, led to higher cash incomes and spending on food. Yet these income gains had a relatively small impact on energy intake and little or no impact on childhood malnutrition. In Kenya and the Philippines, for example, the adoption of cash cropping doubled household income, but children's energy intake rose by only 4–7 percent. Rather than buying more of the same foods, households tended to spend extra income on higher-quality foods and other basic needs.

3. *Increasing access to micronutrient-rich foods.* Early efforts to increase agriculture's contribution to nutrition neglected the role of micronutrients. To help address this

gap, the nutrition community began to engage in agricultural strategies to promote household and community production of micronutrient-rich foods, such as fruits, vegetables, fish, meat, and dairy. These interventions have been shown to effectively increase micronutrient intake and status, especially when combined with effective behavioral change and communication interventions. In northeast Thailand, for example, production of green leafy vegetables in home gardens—combined with social marketing—increased vitamin A consumption among the poor. Some efforts have been less successful, highlighting the need for appropriately designed strategies; there are also likely to be trade-offs between income gains from selling home-produced products and dietary gains from own consumption. Currently, a much larger-scale agricultural approach to micronutrient malnutrition is being developed: breeding micronutrients into staple crops through biofortification. The program is beginning to see some positive nutritional outcomes through the development and dissemination of vitamin A-rich, orange-fleshed sweet potatoes.

4. *Empowering women.* One of the major lessons to emerge from these decades was the critical role women play in providing nutrition to their children. Consequently, efforts were made to increase the participation of women in agricultural development strategies while also recognizing the need to facilitate women's continued involvement in household management and child care. Such strategies have been found effective. For example, a successful intervention from Kenya showed that support for production of orange-fleshed sweet potatoes among women increased consumption, but the nutritional outcomes were greatly improved when accompanied by strategies to promote appropriate child feeding and caring practices.

A Fair Farm Bill for the World

A fair Farm Bill for the international community would include the following:

- Commodity programs that ensure a fair market price for farmers and eliminate export dumping.

- Stronger antitrust enforcement and improved price transparency in the food and agriculture industry could help competition in the global market.

- Support for local food economies, smaller farmers and greater food security would help diversify U.S. cropping systems and reduce agriculture exports.

- A transition to untied, cash-based food aid and a phaseout of sales of food aid (monetization).

The Institute for Agriculture and Trade Policy,
A Fair Farm Bill for the World,
March 6, 2007. www.iatp.org.

There are clearly several pathways through which agriculture can help address undernutrition, but each one has its limitations. To help improve nutrition more effectively, agricultural policies and practices need to foster synergies between the pathways, balancing the contributions of staple foods, micronutrient-rich foods, income, and women, as well as the trade-offs involved. Additional complementary measures are needed to foster links between the agriculture and health sectors to ensure adequate maternal and child care, feeding, and hygiene practices in agricultural households, as well as access to and use of health services.

Challenges and Opportunities for the Future

Over the past 20–30 years, two related processes have had particularly important effects on the linkages between agriculture and nutrition—globalization and urbanization. Processes of globalization have increased the market orientation of the global agrifood system, unleashing new dynamics in food production, trade, and governance. These dynamics have reverberated throughout the food supply chain, affecting not just production, but also the quantity, quality, price, and desirability of food available for consumption. In addition, close to 40 percent of populations in developing countries currently live in urban areas, a figure projected to rise to 60 percent by 2025. In cities, households have different livelihoods: They are less likely to produce their own food, are more dependent on cash income, and have greater access to a wider variety of goods and services. Both women and men work but often become less physically active. Together, globalization and urbanization are altering how agriculture interacts with nutrition in the following ways:

1. *Creating environments conducive to obesity and diet-related chronic diseases.* Globalization and urbanization are associated with greater supply of and demand for energy-dense, nutrient-poor foods, leading to obesity and related diseases in countries that have yet to overcome childhood undernutrition. In Mexico, for example, overweight and obesity among the poor nearly doubled over 10 years to reach 60 percent in 1998, while stunting still affected almost half of the preschoolers from low-income groups. The emergence of this double nutritional burden calls for policy makers to rethink how to use agricultural policy as an instrument for good nutrition. The lesson from the past—that agriculture can best

meet nutritional needs by providing as cheap a source of abundant calories as possible—may no longer be appropriate. For example, Brazil's past policies promoting increases in the production, export, and consumption of soybean oil led to soaring consumption of soybean oil, which today contributes to excessive fat intake in Brazil. Agriculture thus faces a new challenge: ensuring a sufficient supply of staples and micronutrient-rich foods without encouraging excessive consumption of energy-dense, nutrient poor foods.

2. *Elevating the role of agricultural marketing in nutrition linkages.* Earlier efforts to improve the links between agriculture and nutrition focused on production. Today, the more market-oriented nature of agricultural policies means agricultural markets play a more important role in determining food availability and access—a shift reinforced by the role of urbanization in increasing the ratio of market consumers to market producers. One example of this shift concerns horticultural products. Production of fruits and vegetables has increased over recent years, yet inadequate consumption remains a problem worldwide. This gap exists partly because of failures of the market supply chain, such as postharvest losses and lack of market access by small producers, which constrain access and availability. To help address micronutrient deficiencies and chronic diseases, the horticultural and health sectors therefore need to focus not only on production, but also on leveraging and adapting aspects of the market supply chain to make fruits and vegetables more available and affordable for poor households, while also ensuring small producers' access to markets. This challenge applies to the global supply chains linking fruit and vegetable producers in Africa and Latin

America to consumers in Europe and North America, as well as to smaller local markets throughout the developing world.

3. *Increasing the impacts of food and nutritional demands on agriculture.* The greater market orientation of food production and consumption has increased the bidirectional links between agriculture and nutrition: agriculture still affects nutrition, but food and nutritional demands increasingly affect agriculture. It is a twofold process. First, the increasing importance of the cash economy arising from globalization and urbanization is increasing the power of consumers in the marketplace. Second, the rise of the food-consuming industries (processors, retailers, restaurants) is subordinating the power of agricultural producers, especially smallholders. In China, for example, rising incomes, urbanization, and population growth have rapidly increased consumer demand for meat. Demand from supermarkets and restaurants is now growing even faster and includes new demands for volume and specific quality attributes. This situation affects traditional backyard producers of pork (the dominant meat), who have trouble responding to such demands, and large-scale industrial producers, whose share of pork production is rising despite associated negative environmental and health impacts. The challenge for the agricultural sector is to respond to the increasing power of consumers and the food-consuming industries without leaving behind smaller, poorer farmers. At the same time, as diets change, the challenge for the health sector is to encourage consumers—and the food-consuming industries—to demand nutritious foods from agriculture. As past experience has shown, more income and greater market orientation is not always

associated with good nutrition—a lesson reinforced by the rise of obesity and chronic diseases.

Increasing the Synergies Between Agriculture and Nutrition

The changing interaction between agriculture and nutrition in a globalizing and urbanizing world demands new policy responses: old lessons need to be applied and adapted to new realities; emerging challenges and opportunities must be recognized and addressed. To improve the synergies, institutional barriers preventing closer coordination between agrifood and health systems must be broken down. Inflexible governance structures hindered progress in the past and, unless confronted, will continue to do so in the future. At a basic level, capacity building is needed in developing countries to allow more coordinated approaches, while in regional and global institutions, nutritional considerations should become part of multinational agricultural policy making and agricultural considerations should be built into efforts to improve nutrition and health.

> "Small-scale family gardens, school gardens, allotment gardens and urban gardens in unused open spaces should be our strategic counter-attack against the actual food crisis."

Increasing Local Food Production Will Help Alleviate Malnutrition

Willem Van Cotthem

Willem Van Cotthem is an honorary professor of botany at the University of Ghent, Belgium, and a consultant for desertification and sustainable development. In the following viewpoint, he maintains that applying cost-saving technologies to family, school, or urban gardens will encourage poor rural and urban populations to grow their own food and help alleviate malnutrition and food shortages in many areas.

As you read, consider the following questions:

1. What are the general effects of drought on agricultural development and food prices?

Willem Van Cotthem, "Family Gardens, School Gardens and Urban Gardening Against the Actual Food Crisis," *Container Gardening*, May 5, 2008. Reproduced by permission.

2. What specific technological advances in agricultural production does the author discuss as factors that will help solve the global food crisis?

3. Why does the author believe it will be more effective to improve technology and efficiency on smaller, local farms and not large-scale farming operations?

Drought is described as a very important environmental constraint, limiting plant growth and food production. The World Food Program (WFP) has recently indicated drought in Australia as one of the major factors for the difficulty to deliver food aid to millions of people suffering from hunger and malnutrition. Drought is seen as the force driving up wheat and rice prices, which contributes directly to food shortage, social unrest, and disturbances at the global level. Therefore, mitigating drought and limiting water consumption seems to be essential factors for resolving the actual food crisis and to find long-term solutions to malnutrition, hunger and famine, particularly in the drylands.

Application of water stocking soil conditioners, keeping the soil moistened with a minimum of irrigation water, and seeding or planting more drought tolerant species and varieties will definitely contribute to solve the food crisis. Scientists in China and the USA have recently discovered important genetic information about drought tolerance of plants. It was thereby shown that drought tolerant mutants of Arabidopsis thaliana have a more extensive root system than the wild types, with deeper roots and more lateral roots, and show a reduced leaf stomatal density. My own research work on the soil conditioning compound TerraCottem has led to similar conclusions: treatment with this soil conditioner induced enhancement of the root system with a higher number of lateral roots. More roots mean more root tips and thus a higher number of water absorbing root hairs, sitting close to the root meristem. As a result, plants with more roots can better explore the soil and find the smallest water quantities in a relatively dry soil.

As the world's population is growing by about 78 million people a year, it affects life on this earth in a very dramatic way. Droughts have caused a rise of food prices many times before, but the present situation is quite different, because it is based on specific trends and facts: the faster growing world population and a definite change in international food consumption trends and habits.

False Notions Regarding Drought Solutions

Some experts claim that "major investments to boost world food output will keep shortages down to the malnutrition level in some of the world's poorer nations", and that "improving farm infrastructure and technological boosts to farm yields can create a lot of small green revolutions, particularly in Africa".

It seems quite difficult to believe that "major investments to boost the food output" will be able to "keep the food shortages down to the malnutrition level", wherever in this world. Indeed, the world's most famous research institutes have already developed very effective technologies to boost food production in the most adverse conditions of serious drought and salinity. Yet, not one single organization has ever decided, up to now, to use "major investments" to apply such technologies in large-scale programs, which would most certainly change the food situation in the world's poorest nations.

It seems also difficult to believe that "improving farm infrastructure and technological boosts to farm yields" will be able to create "small green revolutions, particularly in Africa". It is not by improving a farm's infrastructure that one will manage drought. Although a number of technological solu-

A Desert in Bloom

After sixteen years of war [in 1991], one might expect to see the all-too-familiar tragic camp scenes. Instead, the Sahrawis [of Western Sahara] have turned the harsh desert of their exile into an enabling environment. In the midst of another drought on the African continent, the Sahara is blooming. In a daily struggle against their bleak surroundings, Sahrawis have planned gardens in their refugee camps as well as inside Western Sahara. Some of the food needs for the camps' 165,000 residents grow out of these small oases of hope. The vegetable gardens are one of many self-supporting programs initiated by Sahrawi exiles.

Three young Sahrawi agronomists direct the agricultural programs. Working with them are Sahrawi technicians in irrigation techniques, soils, and plant protection in desert environs, and older Sahrawis who contribute their traditional knowledge. For Sahrawis who were accustomed to the less extreme conditions of the Atlantic region of the Sahara, wrenching greenery from this arid land of rock and sandy desert must have seemed a preposterous idea when it was broached in 1977. Some fourteen years later, however, the land is well prepared, wells and water pumps are in place, and a permanent Sahrawi workforce has been trained.

Teresa K. Smith de Cherif,
"Oasis of Hope: Sahrawi Refugee Camps in Western Sahara
Bear the Fruits of Self-Sufficiency Amid a Harsh Environment,"
Cultural Survival, *July 31, 1991. www.cs.org.*

tions to boost farm yields have already been developed, only those tackling the drought problems are an option to create significant changes.

Apply Methods to Rural Areas

I do not believe that such changes can be realized at the level of large-scale farms. On the contrary, I am convinced that application of cost-effective, soil conditioning methods to enhance the water retention capacity of the soil and to boost biomass production in the drylands, is the best solution to help the poor rural people to avoid malnutrition and hunger, giving them a "fresh" start with a daily portion of "fresh vegetables". These rural people, forming the group most affected by the food crisis, do not need to play a role in boosting the world's food production. They simply need to produce enough food for their own family ("to fill their own hungry stomach"). Application of cost-effective technologies should therefore be programmed at the level of small-scale "family gardens" or "school gardens" and not at the scale of huge (industrial) farms, where return on investment is always the key factor for survival of the business.

Preferentially, major investments to boost the food output in the drylands should be employed to improve food production in family gardens and school gardens, in order to offer all rural people an opportunity to produce more and better food, vegetables and fruits, full of vitamins and mineral elements, mostly for their own family members or kids, partly for the local market.

Splendid examples of long-term combating food shortage with family gardens can be seen since 2006 in the refugee camps in S.W. Algeria (UNICEF [United Nations Children's Fund] project). One can only hope that such a success story will soon be duplicated in many similar situations, where hungry people wait for similar innovative and well-conceived practices, with a remarkable return on investment, laying solid foundations for further sustainable development.

Recently, a number of initiatives have been taken to enhance urban gardening space, not only with allotment gardens, but also with "guerilla gardening" and transformation of open, underused spaces into small-scale garden plots for downtown dwellers, apartment dwellers, and even for university students like those at the McGill University in Montreal. Many poor urban people are very keen on harvesting their own crops in such small gardens or applying container gardening on balconies, terraces, rooftops or other unused open spaces. Support for urban agriculture or urban gardening can be seen as a priority for decision-makers to reverse the world's food crisis.

Food aid, be it with billions of dollars, can only be very effective if priority is given to local food production for the poor rural or urban people, who can not afford to buy the expensive commercial food products in shops or supermarkets. Small-scale family gardens, school gardens, allotment gardens and urban gardens in unused open spaces should be our strategic counter-attack against the actual food crisis.

> *"Americans have collectively eaten over a trillion servings of food containing one or more GM [genetically modified] ingredients, without a single case of harm."*

Biotechnology Will Help Alleviate Malnutrition

Paul Driessen and Cyril Boynes Jr.

Paul Driessen is senior policy advisor for the Congress of Racial Equality (CORE), Committee for a Constructive Tomorrow, and Center for the Defense of Free Enterprise. He is also the author of Eco-Imperialism: Green Power, Black Death. *Cyril Boynes Jr. is CORE's director of international programs. In the following viewpoint, the authors assert that genetically modified (GM) food is the most effective way to alleviate malnutrition in developing countries and excoriate opponents of agricultural biotechnology as zealots who are violating the rights of the poor and malnourished in these countries to food security and adequate nutrition.*

Paul Driessen and Cyril Boynes Jr., "Facts Versus Fears on Biotechnology," Intellectual Conservative.com, March 8, 2005. Reproduced by permission.

As you read, consider the following questions:

1. According to the authors, what arguments do zealots use to oppose the use of agricultural biotechnology and genetically modified (GM) food?

2. How many acres of GM crops were planted in 2004, according to the viewpoint?

3. What are some of the benefits of GM crops and biotechnology as presented by the authors?

The Congress of Racial Equality's recent conference [in 2005], video and commentary on agricultural biotechnology presented personal testimonials from African farmers whose lives have been improved by genetically modified (GM) crops, impressive data on progress, and a message of hope for poor, malnourished people in developing countries. The response has been overwhelmingly positive.

But not from all quarters. Predictably, anti-GM zealots continue to offer a steady stream of unsupported and unsupportable invective. To hear them tell it, biotechnology is a "scourge" that will do nothing to save lives or reduce poverty and malnutrition. "Evil multinationals" like Monsanto [a multinational agricultural corporation] are determined to impose "a new form of slavery" that will "displace" poor people from their lands.

The fear-mongering would be hilarious, if the hate-GM campaign didn't have such tragic consequences for a world where 800 million people are chronically malnourished, and 3 billion struggle to survive on less than $700 a year. A healthy dose of facts is in order.

Facts About GM Crops

GM crops are created with great care in laboratories, using techniques that are far more precise than anything previously. They are tested repeatedly and are regulated by the EPA [Environmental Protection Agency], FDA [Federal Drug Administration], USDA [United States Department of Agriculture], and other agencies. Americans have collectively eaten over a trillion servings of food containing one or more GM ingredients without a single case of harm. Indeed, as Greenpeace co-founder Dr. Patrick Moore and others have demonstrated, every single claim of risk to people or the environment—from monarch butterfly deaths to destabilized insect ecology, diminished biodiversity and dangers to human health—has been refuted by scientific studies.

And yet, radical groups like Greenpeace and the Sierra Club continue to place ultra-precaution against minor, distant, theoretical risks to healthy, well-fed Westerners above the very real, immediate, life-threatening risks faced by our Earth's poorest and most malnourished people.

Thankfully, despite all the invectives, farmers the world over are increasingly turning to GM technology, planting 200 million acres last year [2004]. They don't for a minute believe ag [agricultural] biotech is a magic bullet that will make them rich or solve the world's hunger problems. But they know it dramatically increases crop yields, farm profits and people's nutrition—while reducing pesticide use, crop losses to drought, insects and disease, and the amount of land that will be needed to feed a world population that is expected to hit 9 billion by 2050, before leveling off.

GM Technology Has Advantages

If the world had to rely on organic farming or 1960s agricultural technologies to produce as much food as it actually did in 2000, notes Dr. Norman Borlaug, Nobel Prize laureate for the first Green Revolution, "we would have had to double the amount of land under cultivation." Millions of acres of forest and grassland habitats would have been slashed, burned and plowed for subsistence farming—or millions more people would have starved. As human populations grow, the problem would only worsen. Instead, thanks to biotechnology, farmers

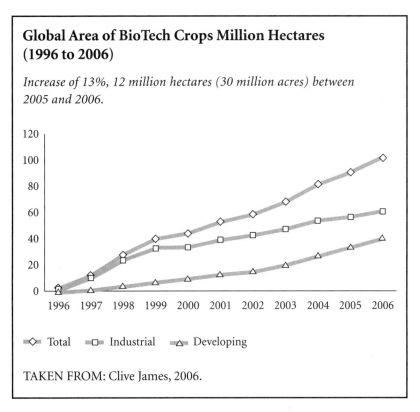

Global Area of BioTech Crops Million Hectares (1996 to 2006)

Increase of 13%, 12 million hectares (30 million acres) between 2005 and 2006.

TAKEN FROM: Clive James, 2006.

can grow far more from the same acreage, thereby preserving habitats and fostering biodiversity and nutrition.

Bt [biotechnology] cotton has allowed Chinese farmers to reduce their pesticide use by 50 to 70 percent—while increasing their yields by 25 to 66 percent, and their incomes by US$300 per hectare (US$120 per acre). Since most of these chemicals were applied via hand spraying, they've also slashed accidental pesticide poisoning. Farmers in India, Africa, and Latin America have had similar experiences.

Bt plants also eliminate pests like corn borers, which chew pathways for dangerous fungal contaminants. They thus reduce rot and waste—and mycotoxins that cause fatal diseases in animals, and cancer, reduced immunity and birth defects in humans. By contrast, organic corn meals purchased right off British supermarket shelves had fumonisin levels up to 50 times higher than conventional or biotech corn—and 20 to 30 times the allowable limits set by UK [United Kingdom] law. Many organic fruits and vegetables also have e-coli bacterial levels sharply higher than conventionally grown crops.

By reducing the need to cultivate for weed control, herbicide-tolerant crops greatly decrease soil erosion (by nearly a billion tons per year), keeping sediment out of lakes and streams. No-till farming also reduces fuel use (by some 300 million gallons of gasoline a year), and increases carbon dioxide uptake by soils—good news for anyone worried about global warming.

Increased crop yields, in turn, mean African farmers can grow enough crops to feed livestock, so they can regularly include protein in their diets for perhaps the first time in their lives.

Anti-GM Activists Reject Facts

But anti-GM activists won't let anything as silly as facts affect their misplaced resolve to stop biotech progress in its tracks. A typical ploy is to portray Canadian farmer Percy Schmeiser as a victim, sued by the villainous Monsanto to enforce its intellectual property rights, after GM crops had "adventitiously appeared" on his land.

It's a compelling story—if you ignore the facts and court decisions. In affirming Schmeiser's conviction for patent violation, Canada's Supreme Court observed that it defied belief that 90 percent of his crop (1,030 acres or 1.5 square miles) was "adventitiously" converted to biotech varieties by seeds or pollen blown in from neighboring fields. As his own field hand testified, Schmeiser had carefully collected and treated seeds from biotech canola grown on a small section of his farm. He then planted those seeds in nine separate fields. He got caught, Monsanto sued, and his phony defense got laughed out of court. "Percy Schmeiser," the court noted, "was not an innocent bystander."

Another Anti-GM Canard

Yet another canard is the claim that modern farming practices will displace farmers. In 1780, over 95 percent of Americans were farmers; today about 3 percent are, and they grow many times more food per acre than their ancestors ever dreamed was possible. Those who abandoned farms were "displaced" to cities. But would their descendents—including urban environmentalists—prefer to give up their modern comforts and return to the era of sunup-to-sundown, back-breaking farm labor?

As Grandmother Driessen used to say, the only good thing about the good old days is that they're gone. Kenya's Akinye Arunga puts it this way: "Cute indigenous lifestyles simply mean indigenous poverty, indigenous malnutrition, indigenous disease and childhood death. I don't wish this on my worst enemy, and I wish our so-called friends would stop imposing it on us."

Unfortunately, radical activists are doing exactly that. They are preventing poor Africans from acquiring modern farming methods, adequate electricity, and pesticides to control malaria. Their callous ideology is certainly an efficient form of "all-natural" population control. But it violates third world people's basic human rights to nutrition, and life itself.

Technology a Boon to Farmers

As to "enslaving" farmers, ag [agricultural] biotech actually frees them from much of the drudgery of subsistence farming. It cuts the time they have to spend in fields, doubles or triples their yields, feeds their families (and their neighbors' families), and puts money in their pockets. As an African Patrick Henry [American revolutionary] might say, If this be slavery, make the most of it.

But the anti-biotech campaigners charge ahead, oblivious to the suffering and malnutrition they are helping to perpetuate, and to the hopes and dreams they are suffocating.

The campaign underscores the adage that nothing in the world is more dangerous than sincere ignorance and conscientious stupidity—except perhaps deliberate eco-manslaughter. No wonder Dr. Moore says the greens' opposition to biotechnology "clearly exposes their intellectual and moral bankruptcy."

> *"Rather than discussing the possibility of using GM [genetically modified] foods in Africa ... leaders should look at ways to develop sustainable farming as a potential solution to the hunger crisis in Africa."*

Biotechnology Is Not the Solution to the Problem of Malnutrition

Stefania Bianchi

Stefania Bianchi is Inter Press Service's European Union correspondent. In the following viewpoint, she outlines the opposition of Consumers International (CI) to the growing genetically modified (GM) food movement in Africa and its claims that GM food is an unproven and untested alternative that detracts from the real issues involved in the food crisis.

As you read, consider the following questions:

1. According to the author, what is the danger of focusing on genetically modified food (GM) in developing African nations?

Stefania Bianchi, "Africa Needs Food Security, Not Experimental Crops," *Global Policy Forum*, July 1, 2005. Reproduced by permission.

2. What is the controversy surrounding GM food in Africa, as outlined by the author?

3. What does Consumers International (CI) propose as an alternative solution to GM food to alleviate food shortages and malnutrition in Africa?

While large biotechnology corporations, and some governments, try to promote genetically modified (GM) crops as a solution to food shortages and malnutrition, Consumers International (CI) insists there is no evidence that GM crops will solve those problems. "Genetic modification will not solve world hunger. The supposed benefits of GM have not been proven to outweigh potential risks to the environment, human and animal health. It would make more sense to put scarce money in other technologies that are more ecologically and economically suited to poor farmers and consumers," Amadou Kanoute, director of CI in Africa said in a statement Wednesday [in 2005].

Food Security Is Key

London-based CI, which works to put consumer rights and social justice at the centre of the international development agenda, is calling for G8 [Group of 8, a forum of the world's major industrialized nations] leaders to focus on food security in Africa. It warns that claims made by biotechnology companies are detracting attention from real causes of hunger in Africa, such as the lack of access to and distribution of food, as well as internal conflict and poor infrastructure. CI says African farmers are faced with unfavourable international trade rules and although they are keen to improve farming methods, the use of GM crops could do more damage than good.

GM crops are created by inserting genes from different plants or even animals into a species to provide it with special attributes, such as resistance to pesticides. The process is completely different from conventional breeding techniques, and has yet to be proven safe. The first major GM food was introduced on the market in the mid-1990s. Since then, GM strains of maize, soybean, rapeseed and cotton have been marketed and traded nationally and internationally in several areas. GM varieties of papaya, potato, rice, squash, sugar beet and tomato have also been released in some countries.

Controversy Erupts over GM Crops

The production of GM crops has increased significantly over the last decade, but the issue has provoked bitter controversy. Supporters say they will increase yields, but opponents argue that they could have unpredictable health risks. Other major concerns are increased control of the food chain by corporations, and misleading claims about solving food supply problems and about the benefits of GM crops to farmers, CI says. At the heart of the problem, adds the organisation, is the fact that GM crops are promoted with "aggressive zeal" by biotech corporations, raising the hopes and expectations of farmers and communities. Unfortunately, CI says, many of the proposed "miracle solutions" end in failure.

"African countries are concerned about bio safety, and the consequences of introducing GM food without proper, independent, human safety evaluations and environmental assessments," David Cuming, GM campaigns manager with CI, told IPS [Inter Press Service]. "At present, African countries do not have the proper regulatory framework in place to cope with GM. Yet they are being pushed very hard by the biotech corporations, and the American government, to introduce it quickly," he added.

CI says GM food is also poorly suited to African farmers in part because it is expensive. "In Africa, farmers save their seeds to use the following year. When they use GM seeds, they are forced to buy them each year so destroying their food pro-

Public Attitudes on Genetically Modified Crops

High levels of public concern about GM [genetically modified] crops exist both in countries where they are grown and in countries where they have yet to be introduced.

A January 2005 poll indicates that 92% of Canadian consumers have "some level of concern" about the long-term risks of GM products on human health. In Britain, public attitudes to GM foods are hardening. Some 61% of those polled in September 2004 by the UK [United Kingdom] consumer association *Which?* expressed concern about GMOs [genetically modified organisms] in food production—up from 56% in 2002.

Surveys in Canada, Australia and elsewhere indicate that up to 90% of consumers say they want labels on GM foods.

A February 2005 EU [European Union] Markets report by Greenpeace states that 49 of 60 top retailers have a no-GM policy for their house brands.

Consumers International, "GMOs: Why Consumers Should Take Action," Fact Sheet, 2005. www.consumersinternational.org.

duction systems. This puts control of the food chain in the hands of a small number of unscrupulous biotech corporations," Cuming said.

An Alternative to GM Crops

Instead of spending millions of dollars on what CI calls "a grandiose biological experiment without a clear idea of how it is supposed to help African consumers", the group says governments and corporations should seek inspiration from alternative solutions. "A large part of food shortages has to do with food distribution and access. Despite what the U.S. government wants people to believe, GM food is not the only food available. If other food is available, shouldn't Africans be able to choose?" Cuming asked.

Rather than discussing the possibility of using GM foods in Africa—a topic that is expected to be included in next week's talks [July 2005]—CI says G8 leaders should look at ways to develop sustainable farming as a potential solution to the hunger crisis in Africa. "This is about making the most of resources that farmers have in order to end poverty in rural areas. There have been several successful sustainable farming developments in Africa, including pest control for maize and drought tolerance in rice," Cuming said.

CI adds that to support African consumers, G8 leaders should act to make markets work more effectively, involve consumers in the development process to ensure their needs are met, and commit funding to implement the recommendations of the Commission for Africa. In March [2005] the commission's report proposed radical steps governments can take to support the development of Africa, such as doubling aid, debt cancellation and trade reform.

Periodical Bibliography

The following articles have been selected to supplement the diverse views presented in this chapter.

Ronald Bailey	"A Tale of Two Scientific Consensuses," *Reason Magazine*, April 6, 2007.
Dara K. Dix	"Recipe for a Hungry Planet," *U.S. Catholic*, October 2007.
Jon Entine	"Let Them Eat Precaution," April 4, 2006. www.aei.org.
Shawn Hattingh	"Liberalizing Food Trade to Death," *Monthly Review*, June 2008.
Kerry Howley	"Demon Seed," *Reason Magazine*, March 28, 2008.
Kathambi Kinoti	"Women Worst Hit By Food Crisis," *Monthly Review*, February 2008.
Andrew Leonard	"It's Monsanto's World, We Just Live in It," *Salon*, February 9, 2006.
Alvaro Vargas Llosa	"Food for Thought," *The New Republic*, April 23, 2008.
Scott Miller and Scott Kilman	"Biotech-Crop Battle," *Wall Street Journal*, November 8, 2005.
John Nichols	"The World Food Crisis," *The Nation*, May 12, 2008.
Brett D. Schaefer, Ben Lieberman, and Brian M. Riedl	"Peanut Paste Treats Malnutrition," *Current Science*, May 2, 2008.
Trevor Snapp	"Fighting Malnutrition One Spoonful at a Time," *National Catholic Reporter*, August 31, 2007.

For Further Discussion

Chapter 1

1. Both Fred Magdoff and Nicholas Eberstadt offer estimates on the number of people worldwide who suffer from malnutrition or lack critical nutrients. Do you agree with Magdoff that global malnutrition is a severe problem? Or do you concur with Eberstadt that although global malnutrition is a problem, it has been exaggerated? Explain.

2. Is malnutrition a severe problem in the United States? After reading the viewpoints by the Food Research and Action Center and Robert Rector and Kirk Johnson, state your position using evidence from the articles.

3. A viewpoint from *The Sustainability Report* contends that obesity and malnutrition are related problems. Do you agree with this reasoning? Why or why not?

4. Deroy Murdock maintains that although obesity is a growing problem, undernutrition is a more serious issue and the World Health Organization should be focusing on that. Do you believe that too much attention and resources are concentrated on obesity? Explain.

Chapter 2

1. After reviewing the argument made by Christine Facciolo, how does aging lead to malnutrition? Do you believe that malnutrition amongst the elderly is a serious problem? Explain your view.

2. Based on the viewpoints presented by Ben Lieberman and Robert Zubrin, do you think our increasing reliance on biofuels is causing malnutrition? In light of our current

energy crisis and the high cost of fuel, should we be using more biofuels? What do you think would be the consequences of this policy?

3. Do you believe that global warming is causing malnutrition, as argued by Sarah DeWeerdt? Or do you concur with the Science & Public Policy Institute's opinion that global warming does not cause malnutrition? Support your view.

4. After reading all the viewpoints in this chapter, what do you believe are the major causes of malnutrition? Explain your answer.

Chapter 3

1. Do you agree that national governments have a key role in fighting malnutrition, as asserted by Oxfam International? Or do you concur with Israel Ortega, that governments should not be responsible for alleviating malnutrition? Explain your answer.

2. Liesbeth Venetiaan-Vanenburg maintains that global partnerships are essential in the fight against malnutrition. Do you agree with this opinion? Why or why not?

Chapter 4

1. How will empowering women help to alleviate malnutrition? After reviewing the viewpoint written by Laura Johnston Monchuk, provide evidence that empowering women will lessen the scourge of global malnutrition.

2. According to the viewpoint written by Corinna Hawkes and Marie T. Ruel, implementing more effective agricultural trade policies will help to alleviate malnutrition. Do you agree with this assertion? Explain your answer.

3. Do you feel like biotechnology—particularly genetically modified (GM) food—is a safe and effective way to address the problem of malnutrition, as argued by Paul

Driessen and Cyril Boynes Jr.? Or, like Stefania Bianchi, do you think that GM food is problematic as a solution? Support your view.

Organizations to Contact

The editors have compiled the following list of organizations concerned with the issues debated in this book. The descriptions are derived from materials provided by the organizations. All have publications or information available for interested readers. The list was compiled on the date of publication of the present volume; the information provided here may change. Be aware that many organizations take several weeks or longer to respond to inquiries, so allow as much time as possible.

Action Against Hunger/Action Contre la Faim (ACF)
247 W. Thirty-Seventh Street, New York, NY 10018
(877) 777-1420 • fax: (212) 967-5480
e-mail: info@actionagainsthunger.org
Web site: www.actionagainsthunger.org

Action Against Hunger/Action Contre la Faim (ACF)works to save lives by alleviating hunger through the prevention, detection, and treatment of malnutrition during and after emergency situations such as conflict, war and natural disaster. ACF employs more than six thousand field workers in forty countries to implement lifesaving programs in nutrition, food security, water and sanitation, health, and advocacy. Its nutritional programs, for example, evaluate nutritional needs, treat and prevent acute malnutrition, provide technical training and support for local staff, and interact with national ministries and governments. ACF publishes two newsletters, *RESPONSE* and *Update Against Hunger,* and publications such as *Women and Hunger: Women Play a Central Role in the Fight Against Hunger* and *Water, Sanitation, and Hygiene Manual for Populations at Risk.*

Bread for the World Institute

50 F Street NW, Suite 500, Washington, DC   20001
(800) 82-BREAD • fax: (202) 639-9401
e-mail: bread@bread.org
Web site: www.bread.org

Bread for the World Institute offers policy analysis on hunger and disseminates research and strategy to its advocacy network, opinion leaders, policy makers and the public about hunger in the United States and abroad. It believes that by educating American citizens about hunger and malnutrition, Americans will be empowered to bring about change. To this end, the Institute publishes an annual report on hunger and frequent briefing papers that provide in-depth analysis of current hunger issues. For example, *Ending Hunger: The Role of Agriculture* examines the impact rising food prices have had on poor communities and stresses the need for more investment in sustainable agriculture and development.

Centers for Disease Control and Prevention (CDC)

1600 Clifton Road, Atlanta, GA   30333
(800) CDC-INFO
e-mail: cdcinfo@cdc.gov

The Centers for Disease Control and Prevention (CDC) is one of the divisions of the U.S. Department of Health and Human Services. In 2000 the CDC created the International Micronutrient Malnutrition Prevention and Control Program (IMMPaCt), which allows the CDC to work with partners such as the United Nations Children's Fund (UNICEF), World Health Organization (WHO), United States Agency for International Development (USAID), and others to aid countries in building national capacity to eliminate micronutrient deficiencies. IMMPaCt trains and supports governments and regional organizations to assess and monitor the level of micronutrient deficiencies; create new partnerships to support micronutrient interventions at the global and national levels; and assist governments and regional organizations to implement systems to monitor the efficacy of intervention programs. IMMPaCt provides a wealth of information on micronutrient deficiencies and micronutrient facts.

Congressional Hunger Center (CHC)
400 North Capitol Street NW, Suite G100
Washington, DC 20001
(202) 547-7022 • fax: (202) 547-7575
Web site: www.hungercenter.org

The Congressional Hunger Center (CHC) is a nonprofit antihunger organization that trains leaders to fight hunger and malnutrition in the United States and around the world. It sponsors and administers the Bill Emerson National Hunger Fellows Program, which trains emerging leaders in the fight to alleviate hunger in the United States. Its international program, the Mickey Leland International Hunger Fellows Program, sends some of the most devoted and talented people working in the field to affected areas in the world to join to work with communities to address issues of hunger and malnutrition. The CHC also publishes the *Sustenance* newsletter, which provides updates on the latest congressional hunger and nutrition policies.

Food Research and Action Center (FRAC)
1875 Connecticut Avenue NW, Suite 540
Washington, DC 20009
(202) 986-2200 • fax: (202) 986-2525
Web site: www.frac.org

The Food Research and Action Center (FRAC) is a nonprofit organization that aims to improve public policies and public-private partnerships in order to alleviate hunger and undernutrition in the United States. FRAC conducts research to ascertain the extent of the hunger and undernutrition in the United States; advocates public policies that will reduce hunger and undernutrition; coordinates public information campaigns on the scourge of undernutrition; and trains and supports a nationwide network of advocates, food banks, policy makers, and program administrators. It also coordinates the Campaign to End Childhood Hunger, which encompasses hundreds of citizen groups working together to address the issue of childhood hunger and nutrition in the United States. FRAC publishes a number of studies on childhood hunger, such as annual reports on school breakfast programs, *School Breakfast Scorecard*, and an annual profile of various food and nutrition programs for children across the country, *State of the States: A Profile of Food and Nutrition Programs Across the Nation.*

International Food Policy Research Institute (IFPRI)
2033 K Street NW, Washington, DC   20006-1002
(202) 862-5600 • fax: (202) 467-4439
e-mail: ifpri@cgiar.org
Web site: www.ifpri.org

The International Food Policy Research Institute (IFPRI) is a subgroup of the Consultative Group on International Agricultural Research, an association of sixty-four governments, private foundations, and international and regional organizations working together to find and implement sustainable solutions to eradicate hunger, malnutrition, and poverty. IFPRI identifies and disseminates information about effective and innovative international, national, and regional agricultural and nutrition programs to help poor and disadvantaged communities alleviate hunger and undernutrition. It works to provide policy makers, program administrators and participants, and advocates with the research and information they need to address the daunting issues of malnutrition and hunger. In recent years, IFPRI has published reports on the world food situation including *The World Food Situation: An Overview*, as well as studies on the effect of agricultural trade policy, ending hunger in Africa, and the connection between women and food security.

Oxfam America
226 Causeway Street, 5th Floor, Boston, MA   02114
(800) 77-OXFAM • fax: (617) 728-2594

e-mail: info@oxfamamerica.org
Web site: www.oxfamamerica.org

Oxfam America is the U.S. branch of Oxfam International, a nonprofit organization that addresses poverty, hunger, and social injustice through advocacy, public education, and emergency assistance programs in twenty-seven countries. In the wake of natural disasters and conflict, such as the Myanmar cyclone in 2008, Oxfam and its partners provide emergency assistance and long-term support and training to assist people get back on their feet. It publishes the *Oxfam Impact* and *Oxfam Exchange*, periodicals that review Oxfam's work and feature the latest news on the organization's campaigns. Several times a year it publishes briefing papers, which provide in-depth studies of Oxfam's policy concerns and advocacy programs.

Save the Children
54 Wilton Road, Westport, CT   06880
(800) 728-3843
e-mail: twebster@savechildren.org
Web site: www.savethechildren.org

Save the Children is an independent organization that works to improve the lives of children throughout the world through literacy, nutrition, and training programs and financial sponsorships. It partners with families to identify and solve the problems their children and communities face, and employs a variety of strategies to help families attain self-sufficiency. In addition, Save the Children provides emergency financial and food aid for children affected by natural disasters, drought, and armed conflict. Because women and children are the most vulnerable to hunger and malnutrition, Save the Children mobilizes communities and partner organizations to address the root causes of food insecurity. It is a member of the International Save the Children Alliance, which is comprised of twenty-eight national Save the Children organizations working in more than one hundred and ten countries to ensure the well-being of children. It publishes a number of studies and reports focusing on the state of children's health, such as *Katrina Response: Protecting the Children of the Storm* and *Three Years on from the Tsunami*.

United Nations Children's Fund (UNICEF)
3 United Nations Plaza, New York, NY   10017
(212) 326-7000 • fax: (212) 887-7465
Web site: www.unicef.org

The United Nations Children's Fund (UNICEF) was established to help children in need all over the world. Since its inception in 1946, UNICEF has implemented nutrition programming aimed at fulfilling every child's right to adequate nutrition through programs in infant and young child nutrition; micronutrients; nutrition security in emergencies; and nutrition and HIV/AIDS. UNICEF utilizes a life-cycle approach, which uses partnerships to create and enhance integrated interventions to maximize effectiveness. It publishes reports and studies in a number of subject areas, such as nutrition, health, gender concerns, water, environment, and sanitation.

World Health Organization (WHO)
Avenue Appia 20, 1211, Geneva 27
  Switzerland
(41 22) 791 21 11 • (fax): (41 22) 791 3111
e-mail: info@who.int
Web site: www.who.int

Established in 1948, the World Health Organization (WHO) is the directing and coordinating authority for health concerns within the United Nations system. It is responsible for providing leadership on global health matters, articulating and disseminating policy options, providing technical support to countries, and monitoring and assessing health trends. WHO operates on a six-point agenda: 1) promoting health development in poor and disadvantaged areas; 2) fostering health security; 3) strengthening existing health services; 4) harnessing research, evidence, and information; 5) enhancing partnerships with governments, international, national, and regional organizations, the private sector, and other UN agencies; 6) improving efficiency and effectiveness of health programs. It publishes WHO regional publications, health journals, the annual *World Health Report,* and in-depth studies on subjects of interest. One of the most recent, *Safer Water, Better Health,* examines the key role clean water and adequate sanitation play in health concerns around the world.

Bibliography

Lindsay Allen and Stuart R. Gillespie
What Works? A Review of the Efficacy and Effectiveness of Nutrition Interventions. Geneva: United Nations, Administrative Committee on Coordination, Sub-Committee on Nutrition, 2001.

Robert Drewett
The Nutritional Psychology of Childhood. Cambridge, MA: Cambridge University Press, 2007.

Don A. Franco
Poverty, Malnutrition, Disease, Hopelessness. South Lake Tahoe, CA: Sierra Publishing, 2007.

Ron Fridell
War on Hunger: Dealing with Dictators, Deserts, and Debts. Brookfield, CT: Twenty-First Century Books, 2003.

Gary T. Gardner and Brian Halweil
Underfed and Overfed: The Global Epidemic of Malnutrition. Washington, DC: Worldwatch Institute, 2000.

Stuart Gillespie, Milla McLachlan, and Roger Shrimpton, eds.
Combating Malnutrition: A Time to Act. Washington, DC: UNICEF, 2005.

Ana Gonzalez-Pelaez
Human Rights and World Trade: Hunger in International Society. New York: Routledge, 2005.

Robert F. Kennedy — *The Gospel According to RFK: Why It Matters Now.* Edited by Norman MacAfee. Boulder, CO: Westview Press, 2004.

George Kent — *Freedom from Want: The Human Right to Adequate Food.* Washington, D.C.: Georgetown University Press, 2005.

Tim Lang and Michael Heasman — *Food Wars: The Global Battle for Mouths, Minds, and Markets.* London: Earthscan, 2004.

Howard D. Leathers and Phillips Foster — *World Food Problem: Tackling Causes of Undernutrition in the Third World.* Boulder, CO: Lynne Rienner Publishers, 2004.

Susan Archibald Marcus — *The Hungry Brain: The Nutrition/Cognition Connection.* Thousand Oaks, CA: Corwin Press, 2007.

Anirudh Prasad — *Alleviating Hunger: Challenge for the New Millennium.* Delhi, India: ISPCK, 2001.

Arthur P. Riley, ed. — *Food Policy, Control, and Research.* New York: Nova Biomedical Books, 2005.

Paul Roberts — *The End of Food.* Boston, MA: Houghton Mifflin, 2008.

Loretta Schwartz-Nobel — *Growing Up Empty: The Hunger Epidemic in America.* New York: HarperCollins, 2002.

Richard D. Semba and Martin W. Bloem, eds.   *Nutrition and Health in Developing Countries.* New York: Humana Press, 2008

Douglas R. Shanklin   *Maternal Nutrition and Child Health.* Springfield, IL: C.C. Thomas, 2000.

Peter Svedberg   *Poverty and Undernutrition: Theory, Measurement, and Policy.* Oxford: Oxford University Press, 2000.

Samuel Hauenstein Swan and Bapu Vaitla, eds.   *Hunger Watch Report 2007–2008: The Justice of Eating: The Struggle for Food and Dignity in Recent Humanitarian Crises.* Ann Arbor, MI: Pluto Press and Action Against Hunger, 2007.

United Nations World Food Programme   *Hunger and Health.* London: Earthscan, 2007.

Lyman W. Vesler, ed.   *Malnutrition in the 21st Century.* New York: Nova Science Publishers, 2007.

Christopher Wanjek   *Food at Work: Workplace Solutions for Malnutrition, Obesity, and Chronic Diseases.* Geneva: ILO, 2005.

Brian Wansink   *Marketing Nutrition: Soy, Functional Foods, Biotechnology, and Obesity.* Urbana, IL: University of Illinois Press, 2005.

Diana Wylie   *Starving on a Full Stomach: Hunger and the Triumph of Cultural Racism in South Africa.* Charlottesville, VA: University Press of Virginia, 2001.

Index

A

ActionAid, 128

Afghanistan, 81

Africa
  AIDS, 79
  conflicts, 77, 78–79
  food insecurity, 75, 76, 78–79, 129–130, 199–203
  genetically-modified food, debate, 193, 197–198, 199, 200, 201–203
  global warming's effects, 112, 116
  humanitarian aid, 165
  infectious diseases, 58–61
  rice consumption and agriculture, 14–15, 203
  See also specific countries

Aging, and nutrition, 64, 85–92

Agribusiness. *See* Commercial agricultural production

Agricultural production. *See* Production levels, food

Agricultural technology
  biotech will help alleviate malnutrition, 192–198
  biotech will not help alleviate malnutrition, 199–203
  energy, 25, 196
  irrigation projects, 112, 187, 189
  production increases, 15, 108, 112, 116, 153, 179, 187–190, 193, 194, 201
  rice crops, 15, 116
  wells, 60–61, 189
  See also Biofuels

Agricultural trade. *See* Trade

Aid
  cash, 131, 181
  effectiveness, 129–132, 191
  grain, and ill effects, 152
  nutrition intervention, 164–165, 166–171
  organization types, 127–128
  world donation totals, 149
  See also Government programs; International governmental organizations (IGOs); Nongovernmental organizations (NGOs)

AIDS crisis, 79

Alcohol abuse, 89

Americans, quality of life, 43–45

Anemia, 72

Argentina, 154

Asociacion de Mujeres Rurales des Uruguay (AMRU), 175–176

Australia, 109, 187

B

Basic crops. *See* Staples

Basic needs, 22, 37, 157

Bennett, Merrill K., 32–33

Bianchi, Stefania, 199–203

Biofuels, 65
  contribute to malnutrition, 98–103
  do not cause malnutrition, 104–110
  effects on food prices, 24–25, 100–102, 103, 106–109

Biological demand, 22–23